Pathmasters for Microbusiness - Mentors, Coaches, Experts & Angels

A Micropreneur's Guidebook

by

Jack W. Savidge

Artist.... Marglo
Publisher ... MicroPreneur Guidebooks, Jack Savidge & Co., La Jolla California

EC and Library of Congress Catalog Data:
ISBN: 1481946455
ISBN-13: 9781481946452

TITLE: PATHMASTERS for MICROBUSINESS MENTORS, COACHES, EXPERTS & ANGELS

Author: Jack Savidge
Subject Keywords: entrepreneur, micropreneur, small business enterprise (SME), mentor, risk and reward, proof of concept, coach, angel investor

TABLE OF CONTENTS

CHAPTER THIRTEEN: **THE ANGELS**

APPENDIX FOUR

Introduction To Your Journey

ALL BUSINESSES EVERYWHERE begin life with a micropreneur pursuing a commercial vision. A microenterprise is a business entity having less than five, or less than 10, or no employees. A micropreneur is someone who works alone or leads a team of microventurers.

Did you know microenterprises dominate all worldwide economies, accounting for 98% of all existing businesses? You, then, are one of almost 200 million small engines that power global commerce. Over 80% of microventures are sole proprietorships, operating with no employees. Those with less than five employees have an average of two employees while those with less than 10 employees have an average of six employees.

All enterprises start with promise, but over 50% do not survive the first five years. Those that do survive reward the micropreneur with a meager existence. These are the facts. No matter how small or large, the enterprise competes in a thin slice of present and future commerce reshaped by inescapable change. Are there means to increase your probability of reward? Yes.

How do we do that? Easy, by reaching beyond our own knowledge and experience in order to manage, sustain and grow our enterprise.

Building an idea into a microenterprise is a hard and often lonely journey. We work to create and profitably sell and deliver unique products and services to meet the relentless change of customers' perception of value. We strive to enrich our customers, employees, suppliers, investors, family, community, nation, and ourselves. We struggle to survive among competition and changing market demands. We devise and implement sales programs to create and serve new customers. Finally, we measure, enrich and retool our personal and business strengths.

The Micropreneurial Leader

All micropreneurs have common traits. They have a sense of urgency and are energetic, skilled, independent, authoritarian, suspicious, and charismatic people taking business risks for future reward. Many of you, however, are reluctant to reach beyond your own self-reliance to ask others for advice to build a sustainable small business.

This guidebook will encourage you to seek experienced outsiders –Mentors, Coaches, Experts or Angels - who are "PathMasters." These helpful outsiders are microenterprise tested and experienced as they listen, have the know-how to show-how, can find answers, and like to invest money in passionate people with valuable ideas. Once connected to a PathMaster, you will gain the confidence necessary to move closer to your microenterprise vision of success.

My Book Reader

This guidebook is written specifically for founders and owners of micro or very small enterprises. Who will benefit? Solo consultants, doctors, hair stylists, service tradespeople such as plumbers and carpenters, retail shop owners, technical start-up engineers and artisans making and selling their crafts. The book is especially useful for people who may be shutout of the job market and are seeking income by starting or running a micro business, and for young people entering the commercial world.

The book instructs microventurers on the value of using a PathMaster to help their enterprise succeed. Descriptions of each PathMaster's unique skills, personality, communication style and work ethic will help readers to identify which PathMaster to engage for their specific business needs.

The book also is a guide for current and potential PathMasters who want to learn how to work more effectively with a micropreneur and his or her team members. Each PathMaster has a distinctive role and assisting style. To be effective, PathMasters must gain new perspectives about micropreneurs by finding out their hopes and fears, their goals and why they behave and manage the way they do.

The guidebook uses clear, practical language to describe simple methods to connect a microenterprise and a PathMaster. It explains how each PathMaster and micropreneur works together. All is combined with my experience into easy-to-read information, along with helpful diagrams, charts, and checklists.

ABOUT THE AUTHOR

MOST CULTURES REGARD talking about yourself as rude and not acceptable. The content of this book comes from my own personal experience, and is not from other authors, published research or surveys. The viewpoints are formed from my diverse business ventures: selling products door-to-door to serving as president of many enterprises; moving from microenterprise founder to angel investor; growing from protégé to mentor; and learning from other PathMasters how to be a coach, expert and angel. Here is a brief overview of my career path:

> in 1950, a route salesperson for a large meat packer selling to butcher shops and restaurants.

> in the 1960's, at 3M Company moved from a desk clerk to the first titled "Marketing Manager" of a major division.

➤ in 1969, with my family of six and no business prospects, risked leaving the safety of a big company to start a micro consulting business.

➤ in 1970, a failing hardware microenterprise hired me as president to create a unique product and identify new customers, secure venture capital and build a team. Three years later, it was profitable and then sold, gaining a high return for the investor's risk capital.

➤ in 1974, co-founded a non-profit firm to assist local underserved and physically and socially disadvantaged micropreneurs. The enterprise excelled in delivering its mission for 23 years.

➤ in the early 1980's, working for a leading venture capital firm, I searched for regional entrepreneurs with investment-worthy ideas. I still invest my resources in talented people with good ideas.

➤ during 40 plus years, was a PathMaster to hundreds of microenterprises and also served as a Board of Director member for more than 25 small and emerging enterprises.

So, join me now to share "lessons learned" about microenterprises and PathMasters - Mentors, Coaches, Experts and Angels. The common sense insights, practical personal growth approaches, tools, and communication styles will help you to succeed and grow.

CHAPTER ONE

NEW HELP IS ON THE WAY

"**I**T IS LONELY RUNNING A COMPANY" or "There is nobody I can talk to!" Every micropreneur often repeats these words and complains of carrying all business burdens alone. Why? The fact is small business owners are lonely. It is difficult to talk about problems with a team, friends, or even those saying they too understand your concerns. Solution: you must find and talk with the right people about how to grow your business.

"I would ask others but my business is different" is the myth often argued by entrepreneurs and small company managers. Maybe you have said this as well. You may believe your customers, marketplaces, products or services, and ways you

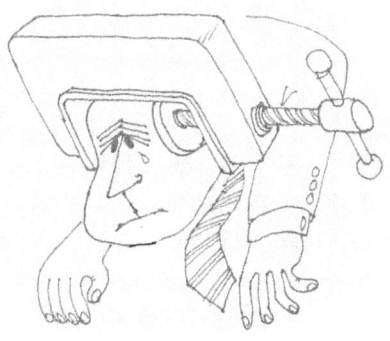

make things are very different from any other vendor. If your enterprise is that different or unique, who else but you could possibly relate to your business? If you are convinced it is useless to take time to talk to anyone, you may be wrong.

My view is:

> all business problems and solutions are the same but some vary by marketplace, service or product value, industry language, and how many zeros measure revenue.

> a small, new enterprise makes its journey over the same paths walked by all entrepreneurs who have gone before. There are no shortcuts to avoid the twists and turns to survival and future success or failure.

> persistence and prudent opportunistic risk-taking create higher odds of achieving success - not intellect, money or luck.

Business is not usually fair! Entrepreneurs and managers make the business journey a burden by seeing unfairness in what are normal situations. Do any of these experiences seem familiar?

> Suppliers are unfair. Because you are a young company, they want cash or very quick payment

for orders placed with them. Then, they sometimes ship your orders late.

› Employees are unfair. They spend time worrying about being paid and talk more about job security instead of doing their work. They want small ownership in the company or some share of the business profits

› Customers are unfair. They ordered your service or product, and you delivered. Now they want a refund or refuse to pay the invoice because of one quality problem and do not order from you again. All you want is one more chance.

› Competition is unfair. You studied marketplace prices for similar services or products and then priced your offerings at a fair customer value. Immediately, competition reduced their prices to almost your costs. Then they hired away key people you wanted to keep to help your business grow.

› Banks or investors are unfair. They told you they had a long-term outlook, yet they offer higher interest rates and a shortened loan or investment period.

Maybe it is unfair but that is business!

"I Can Do it By Myself"

I know you would like to be in full control of your business matters. But believe this, no one has built a business beyond a few employees by making all the decisions themselves. Finding, connecting to, trusting, and using specific expertise is most important to insure the right path to survival and growth.

"How can you be so sure, Jack?" Well, I have been where you are and have lived your responsibilities. I too thought I could manage every business challenge, but I could not. Yes, alone you or I can grow a tiny company into just a small one. But is that really our vision and is it worth all the effort?

When you share and use the unique strength of others to help lift the enterprise, here is what happens. The business creates good products and services for demanding customers. Your committed employees achieve their potential. Finally, your success rewards all those who invested time, support and money so you could achieve your dream. "O.K., who should I work with to help me?"

PathMasters - that is who. They serve as your mentor, coach, expert, and financial angel. I call them PathMasters, as the first part of the word, Path, describes the winding, uphill and downhill trails a business must take on its growth journey. The previous steps of micropreneurs have worn down these twisting new venture routes. PathMasters have traveled to where you want to go. They have wisdom from their own small business experience. They will help you read the trail signs and suggest best paths to take.

Now the second part of the word, Master, describes a very skilled person. Think of a Master mechanic or craftsman, a BandMaster, a SchoolMaster, or BrewMaster. For centuries ship Masters sailed uncharted waters to discover and carry risk-taking settlers to new lands. TrailMasters led pioneers through dangerous, infertile and forbidding lands toward survival. Often in our early enterprise stages, we rely upon earnest but inexperienced associates to help find and track our unique path. PathMasters, however, have practical, broad, and deep expertise and real business experience. When you find your particular PathMaster, you can select the right tools to build your business' future.

You and your small enterprise are on a unique voyage, a long journey, a caravan, an expedition into new frontiers. It is a frightening unknown, and a risk-filled maze of paths not on anyone's map. PathMasters know a great deal but they have NOT walked the exact path you will take. They have not climbed over specific barriers and obstacles you will encounter nor measured the resources needed to reach your destination. PathMasters have, however, walked hundreds of small enterprise paths, coached even the weakest to go the distance, detected trail danger, showed how to course-correct, and encouraged new believers in your vision to provide the necessary funding or talent provisions for the journey.

"What does a PathMaster do?" PathMasters offer their skills as mentors, coaches, experts and financial angels. They can help in different ways. As you read on, you will learn how to find, work with, and communicate with each of them. So, will they guarantee a safe and swift business journey? No, but early on your journey, you must consider PathMasters the best guides.

"Which PathMasters should I use?" Here is my example. To repair my car I may crawl underneath to tighten a bolt. Oh no, I do not have the right size wrench. I do not say, "I'm under the car and have the wrong tool. Can  you help me?" Rather, I must say "Please hand me the #10 wrench" to describe the right tool. Just as any tool will not fit the bolt to fix the car, knowing what kind of PathMaster you need is necessary for solving your specific business challenges. For example, if you need:

> marketplace and customer facts - *get an Expert*

> store or factory operations to run more efficiently - *get a Coach*

> start-up money or to buy more inventory - *get an Angel*

> advertising or selling strategy help - *get an Expert*

> share my concerns to someone I can trust - *get a Mentor*

Look for the right PathMaster in the toolbox of outside resources.

Here are some examples of what a mentor, coach, expert or angel can do:

A Mentor can:

> Listen to and discuss your business plans.

> Provide honest ways to make your team efficient.

> Confidentially evaluate and objectively discuss your ability to lead your team.

A Coach can:

> Train your team to more effectively close a sale.

> Show your employees how to improve delivered quality of your products or services at a lower cost.

An Expert can:

> Suggest more competitive pricing.

> Compile potential customer lists, whether local, national, or global.

An Angel can:

> Suggest ways to increase cash flow.

> Affirm your credit worthiness to a major supplier.

PathMasters are confident of their expertise. They want to and can help. I like to say, "They have the answers, but they just do not know what the questions are." Take the time, think about your critical needs, and then reach into the PathMaster toolbox to choose the right person to lend you an ear and give you a hand.

These outsiders may not be part of your company but they are part of your business community. We tend to build walls around our enterprise for fear someone may learn too much about our business. Being careful is good but too often our business cannot grow beyond the edges of the wall. The word "outsiders" seems negative, like aliens, barbarians and those trying to see or hear something they should not. Be positive. PathMasters are those standing at your door to share the reality that is beyond the wall, to show better ways to solve problems, to offer information about business, and to uncover money to sustain growth of your small firm.

CHAPTER TWO

MEET THE PATHMASTERS!

NOW LET US UNDERSTAND the distinctive expertise and the value each PathMaster offers to help meet your challenges.

Meet the Mentor

Several dictionaries define a Mentor as "a person who acts as guide and adviser to another person, a close trusted and experienced counselor or guide, who, because they are detached and disinterested (unbiased), can hold up a mirror to us."

The legendary young King Arthur of England had a mentor named Merlin the Magician. Alexander the Great had a mentor named Socrates. Famous politicians, athletes, entertainers, and business leaders describe their mentors as playing a critical role in their lives.

Mentors know how to listen, ask the right questions, and then offer wise and practical alternatives for you to consider. You too can benefit from a mentor.

Meet the Coach

The dictionary states "a coach is one who instructs or trains; to train intensively by detailed instructions, frequent demonstrations, and repeated practice; prompting those to be coached to try."

Coaches trained us to play as a team. Our coaches knew, and we trusted they knew, how-to prepare us to compete and excel. They were tough but caring, urging our performance to be the very best at baseball, soccer, and track contests. They were musical band directors, skiing, sailing and art instructors. They were the master mechanics at auto repair garages where we worked, sales managers, production supervisors and

book editors. A coach was anybody having skills we lacked but wanted to learn. They were willing to show us how to grow.

Coaches know how to make things work better. They teach,

show, and train using the tricks of the trade and experienced proven methods.

Meet the Expert

The dictionary describes experts as "very skillful; having much training and knowledge in some special field."

 An expert knows the real facts. They understand a customer's wants and needs, what competitors are doing, where to get the right materials, new team members and money investors. In a lifetime you and I could not collect, classify and correctly use the detailed information they command. This PathMaster has or can quickly find answers to our questions.

Experts know local, regional, and global facts, business operating processes and most importantly, the marketplace. You ask, they tell.

Meet the Angels

The dictionary defines an angel as "a person who provides money for the production of goods and services; a financial backer of an enterprise." This PathMaster is a venture capitalist, banker, private investor, government grantor, or a family member or friend. No need to detail

what an angel does - they invest, sell, or lend money.

Angels know how much money it takes to grow an enterprise. They supply you with capital until your success vision, from their point of view, no longer seems attainable.

No one person has just the right answers for your business. Yes, listen to your brother or sister in-law, university professor, government specialist and spouse as they may have their own ideas about how to make your business work better. Then, rely on Pathmasters to bring practical, objective, experienced-based answers and suggestions to support your actions.

CHAPTER THREE

Your Business Life Cycle

FOUNDING MICROPRENEURS MUST PREPARE to move from each enterprise life stage to the next. What that means is you must know where the company is today. Then you must create a vision of where you want it to go tomorrow. Finally, you must make a plan of how you are going to get the business there. No longer is it possible for any enterprise, large or small, to just randomly walk into the future and survive.

Simple Strategy Tools

Focus, focus, focus is the chant to success. Market-based strategic moves are the keys to success. I will accept that right now your company does not have time for strategic thinking and that you and your team do not believe strategic thinking is needed. Take a minute to look at new thinking tools to make strategic decisions.

First Tool – See Reality

It is hard to confirm the practical truth of what is really happening with your business. Our perceptions may tell us one thing, the reality maybe quite different. To make the point, look at the image below and decide whether you are seeing spirals or circles.

PERCEPTION vs REALITY

Spirals or circles?

Confident you know the answer? Look again to make sure your perception is the reality. They are circles that appear as spirals. Remember this image every time you believe you know what is happening.

Strategy and planning must always begin with honest and realistic answers to these three questions:

1. Where are we now?
2. Where do we want to go?
3. How are we going to get there?

Second Tool - New Product or Service Decisions

Use this tool when defining "where do we want go" and "how are we going to get there." These questions will focus your thinking: Is it Real? Can We Win? and Is It Worth the Effort?

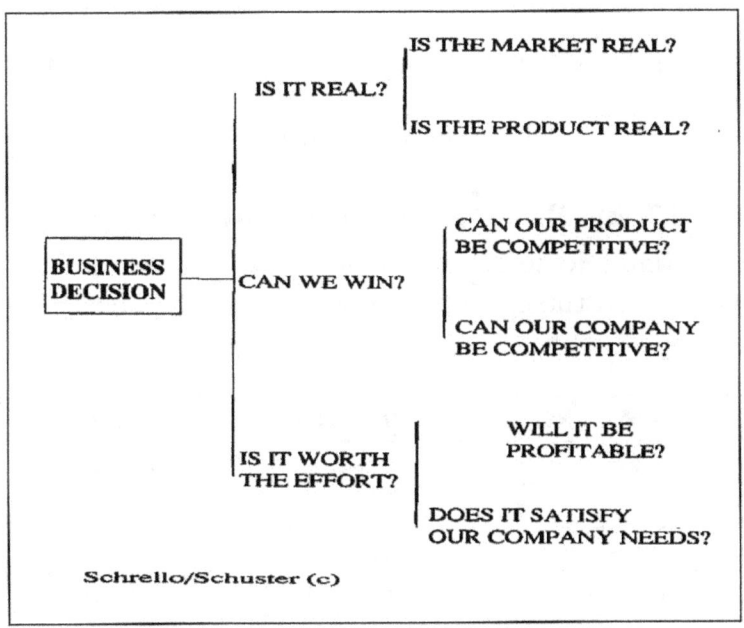

IS THE MARKET REAL?

IS IT REAL?

IS THE PRODUCT REAL?

BUSINESS DECISION

CAN WE WIN?

CAN OUR PRODUCT BE COMPETITIVE?

CAN OUR COMPANY BE COMPETITIVE?

IS IT WORTH THE EFFORT?

WILL IT BE PROFITABLE?

DOES IT SATISFY OUR COMPANY NEEDS?

Schrello/Schuster (c)

Next time you must decide on action for any new technical, manufacturing or market initiative, carefully consider each branch of this business decision tree.

Bring your team together and objectively and openly discuss:

> Do customers consider our products or services better than the competition's?

> Do we really offer better value at a fair price?

> Are we working as hard and as smartly as we could?

> Do we have time to do things right the first time?

> How do we fix what needs fixing?

Third Tool - Personal and Enterprise Life Cycles:

It is simple to compare personal and business life activity. Find in the chart below where your business is and then advance to the next stage.

BUSINESS CYCLE	PERSONAL	AT WORK
New Ideas	Crawling	Chaotic
1st Orders	Walking	Exciting
2nd Orders	Youngster	Validating
New Buyers	Teenager	Organizing
New Products/Services	Young Adult	Growing

Market Owner	Grown-Up	Maturing
Harder to Compete	Elder	Declining
Old Products/Services	Aged	Defensive

The MicroEnterprise Life Cycle - Birth to Death

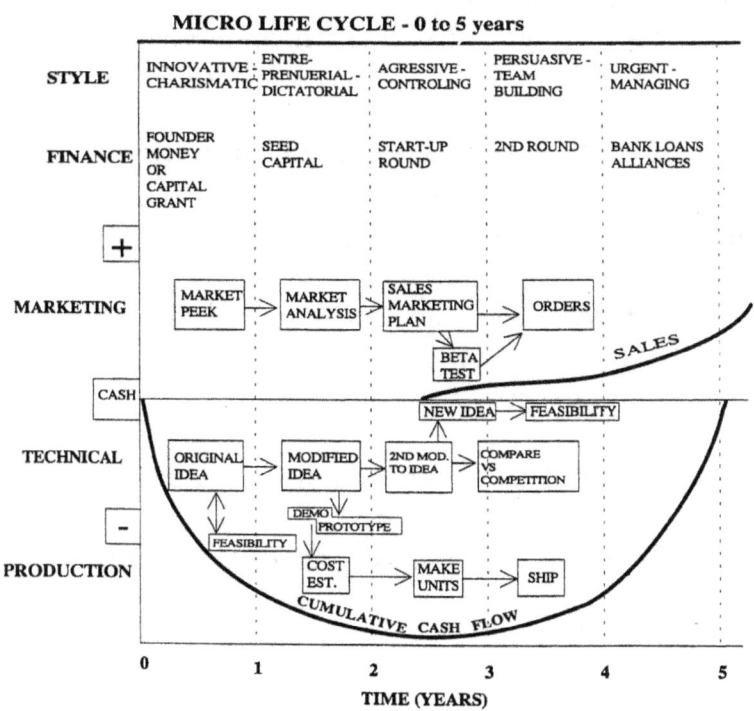

Your business has a finite life span. Throughout each life stage, you will use vital skills to meet the critical growth barriers and perils. It's not the destination that matters; it's how you make the journey.

Let us magnify those first five years of enterprise life. Look at the diagram below. See how the management "style" changes and complements the events occurring in finance, marketing, technical and production.

The twists and turns of the life cycle path require course corrections to reach strategic goals. Working together, micropreneurs and PathMasters cause the new hurdles to decrease and the enterprise value to increase.

Fourth Tool - Make the Most of Your Time

Customer demands, team issues and paperwork! Which one do I fix first? Here is an easy way to prioritize. Review your task lists, calendar events, messages to answer, and so on. Now label each item:

> **Vital** (to sustain the business' life)

> **Essential** (what is of utmost importance)

> **Important** (what needs immediate attention)

> **Trivial** (what is not really necessary)

You must only focus on moving your enterprise from idea to sales, as increasing the number of satisfied customers and profitability requires managing how you spend your time. So, do the Vital tasks until they are completed. Then complete the Essential jobs. Ask others to execute the Important items. Forget the Trivial ... there is no time for them!

To Make Success Happen

Believe this. From now on, it will be harder to survive and flourish in an increasingly competitive world. Your job is to: (1) create more valued products or services, (2) provide customers what they need and will buy, (3) make your offerings available where customers will buy, (4) fight to get and keep customers, (5) motivate employees to satisfy customers, (6) produce profits and cash.

One More Strategic Item

O.K., you have decided on a short-term plan for your enterprise. The chart below takes you beyond tomorrow. Study it and make commitments for longer-term actions when you get there.

EVENT	ACTIONS TO TAKE
Orders	Worship Your Customers
Resources	Get Money, Ideas & People Now
Markets	1st Sell Local, then Nearby
Price	Buy Low and Sell High
Delegate	Build A Team – Let Them Do It
Morale	Get Passionate – They Will Follow
Opportunity	Consider All Ideas – Carefully Take a Risk
New Products	Better Your Own - Before They Do
Partnering	In a Niche Market - Make a Friend

Make this a poster or screen saver where you and your team can see it every day!

CHAPTER FOUR

THE VISION AND MISSION

IT IS TIME TO think big about your enterprise. So, let us put a "vision" umbrella over future growth events. Your team, family and investors want to hear simple and compelling words from you to ignite their excitement. Beyond today, what do you see that they cannot? Where is the business' future? What does it look like? If they can just get an idea of your vision, they will follow. You then must create mental images of that future and the pathway to get there.

No one can predict the future. Now, here is the reality: ordinary people simply cannot describe a vision. We try but the words sound odd, beyond understanding or too outrageous even for our own ears. However, we must keep at it because reaching for a vision pulls us beyond today. Strategic thinking is imagining futures beyond the present. Strategic planning attaches numbers to reasonable future assumptions.

Follow how the thinking flows upward from where you are (OBJECTIVES) to where you want to go (VISION). The results on the way up show how clear and convincing vision possibilities can be.

ACME ENVIRONMENTAL CONTROL, LTD.

VISION
Free the Urban World of Mice

MISSION
Safely exterminate mice in
residential or commercial structures.

STRATEGY
Supply proprietary
rodent lures and mechanisms
to cause a 95% plus death rate.

GOALS
Only use unique natural rodent attractants.
Develop rodent selective paralysis or dying mechanisms

OBJECTIVES
Commission natural lure research.
Test competitive lures and kill mechanisms.
Gain use approvals, patents

Strategic thinking is vital for a young enterprise. It hardens and communicates the micropreneur's dream to all involved. Everyone is aligned to the time, money and talent required to manage and maximize new opportunities. Lastly, it is the catalyst to restart and confidently energize everyone when previous plans just do not work out.

> **VISION IS THE ART OF SEEING THE INVISIBLE**
> – Jonathan Swift, 1711

Someone must artfully see beyond the visible. That someone is you.

CHAPTER FIVE

THE RISKS AND REWARDS

The Micropreneur's Balancing Act

Business is the prudent management of risk and reward. What do the words risk, reward, and prudent mean?

Risk - "a chance or possibility of danger, loss, injury, or other adverse consequences."

Reward - "a return or recompense for service or merit."

Prudent - "careful to avoid undesired consequences," "capable of exercising sound judgment in practical matters," or "sensible, not rash."

Prefer Reward to Risk but carefully measure both with Prudence.

Look at risk, reward, and prudence this way:

"RISKS ARE TAKEN FOR SUCCESS WHEN THE PERCEIVED REWARDS FOR SUCCESS ARE GREATER THAN THE PERCEIVED RISKS OF FAILURE. PERCEPTIONS OF THE TWO ARE MEASURED WITH PRUDENCE." – Jack Savidge

Each person has unique, natural, experiential or survival responses to risk-taking for rewards. All local, regional, or national cultures react differently to the consequences of risk. So, prudently weigh and balance business risk with the perceived rewards for self, family, employees and community.

Micropreneurs and Cultures

Some societies applaud and encourage risk-taking to build wealth. Many cultures envy the successful who amass possessions, while others reject creators of wealth. Many cultures shame those who fail even though they tried their best. Many are cruel and unforgiving until all who suffered from another's failure are repaid. Few societies urge those who failed to "try again."

Cultural perceptions of wealth and financial failure define the limits of micropreneurial risk and reward. Ask your family, team, community leaders and company supporters whether your vision and goals are within the prudent and acceptable risk and reward boundaries.

Risks and Rewards

Key Personal Risk Factors in growing any sized enterprise include:

> - you give up family time for the company.

> - your failure ruins finances.

> - your wealth may change your community status.

> - your business stress harms your health.

> - your reputation is in jeopardy all the time.

Key Personal Rewards by growing any sized enterprise include:

> - freedom to run your own life and time.

> - pride of creating a business family.

> - community service by creating new jobs.

> - personal accomplishment and growth.

> - improved standard of living.

> - recognition by peers and family.

Expected Financial Rewards include:

> for a Micropreneur - above average income, enterprise ownership.

> for an Employee - reasonable income, worker benefits, and enterprise ownership.

> for the Community - increased revenue from more worker taxes.

Expected Psychological Rewards include:

> satisfaction - providing for yourself and employees.

> accomplishment - making your vision come true.

> self-confidence - mastering uncertainty.

> thrill of the game - meeting the challenges and winning.

American president Theodore Roosevelt said it best about an entrepreneur's risking for reward.

"It is not the critic who counts, not the man who points out how the strong man stumbled or where the doer of deed could have done better. The credit belongs to the man who is actually in the arena. Whose face is marred by dust and sweat and blood. Who strives valiantly. Who errs and comes short again and again. Who knows the great enthusiasms, the great devotions, and spends himself in a worthy cause. Who, at the best, knows in the end the triumph of high achievement. And, who, at the worst, if he fails, at least fails while daring greatly, so that his place shall never be with those cold and timid souls who know neither victory nor defeat."

So, is the risk worth it? Only you can make that judgment.

CHAPTER SIX

Who Are Believers?

"WHATEVER THE MIND BELIEVES, the body achieves" but who must believe? The list is short. YOU must believe. Then as your passion and leadership captivate your family, employees, customers, suppliers and investors, they become believers. We all want to believe in those who dare.

First, YOU must believe:

> your enterprises' future vision, mission, and goals

> your working plans for products or a service

> your ability to serve markets from a strong competitive position

> your persistence to quickly satisfy changing customer demands

- your forecasts are reasonable

- your success milestones are realistic

- your determination to make it happen is firm

Second, YOUR FAMILY must believe:

- wholeheartedly supporting your vision is vital

- achieving the vision will better their lives

- growing an enterprise means sacrificing time, energy, and money

Third, YOUR EMPLOYEES must believe:

- their lives are bound to your vision

- their work quality helps attract the right investors as new customers

- their loyalty leads to new coworkers, and future growth opportunities

- their skills, decisions, and extra effort build a strong team

- their benevolent dictator, YOU, manages that way to ensure progress

> their sacrifice of extra time, energy and income is necessary to get the enterprise "up and running"

Fourth, YOUR CUSTOMERS, SUPPLIERS, and INVESTORS must believe:

> your vision, focus, and energy will benefit their business

> your offerings and business practice meet their needs and wants

> your enterprise creed is to support them

People build a business. People need and want images of how to achieve their dreams of success. Everyone connected to the business must be believers. You, and only you, must constantly create and re-ignite believers.

CHAPTER SEVEN

I CAN DO IT MYSELF, THANK YOU!

MOST PERSISTENT PEOPLE CAN start and build a tiny or maybe a small business. Ninety-nine percent of the world's businesses are tiny. They stay tiny because the business owner, unknowingly, wants to control all the day-to-day operations. Picture the tiny business as a playground sandbox with the owner sitting in its center placing all the business operations, like toys, just within grasp. The sandbox cannot become larger as the toys would then be out of reach. That is what can happen if you do not allow others help you make the business sandbox bigger. There is nothing wrong with a tiny business, but usually the owner takes home about what they would earn working for someone else, there are few employees and no real community impact. For some, this reward is acceptable.

Typical micropreneur attitudes and beliefs are:

> I started the business and, while a challenge, I will continue to manage it as mine.

> Solving business problems is solely my business.

> My enterprise information is not open to outsiders and I do not have time to educate anyone about how the enterprise does or does not work.

> The business environment keeps changing but by trial and error, maybe we will make it.

Risky beliefs! Holding these convictions causes inefficiency, misdirected energy, money, missed market opportunities, lowered employee morale, investor impatience and less future profit. Good luck with that!

"O.K., what problems are so big I cannot figure them out by myself?" you may say.

My answer? When you are managing these Vital or Essential issues:

> deciding which key people to hire and let go.

> confronting a founding partner to say, "It is time for you or me to go."

> running out of time to do everything.

- delegating to find no one is competent enough to do the job.

- realizing to grow a business means losing absolute control.

- meeting payroll by somehow finding new money.

- understanding that you do not understand your markets.

- knowing to move forward demands new skills.

- changing behavior to meet each new business evolution.

- equipping employees for the next business phase.

- justifying why the business interferes with your family life.

- guessing about market or product/service costs.

- knowing bookkeeping and workflow is out of control.

So, think about it, and maybe, just maybe you will realize you cannot manage it all by yourself.

CHAPTER EIGHT

What, Tell Them My Secrets?

MAKE LIFE EASIER FOR yourself by forgetting the business myth that everything behind your front door is secret. Next, assume the minute you talk about or show your product or service to anyone, competitors probably already know about it or soon will. The practical way to manage your information is not talking about anything you do not want anyone to know right now.

Follow this rule when talking about your business: **Anyone can ask you an indiscrete question, but only you can respond with an indiscrete answer.**

Telling outsiders your business story attracts new believers. They are intrigued when hearing about where you are and where you are going. Often these conversations cause real excitement. You sense their interest in joining you in some way to help move the business forward. Be open to letting others into your circle, but be prudent in what you tell them. These "outsiders" may be PathMasters with skills and expertise to help you. Take the first step to risk by inviting them into your confidence.

Can You Trust a PathMaster?

In general, yes. PathMasters keep their customer's information private. For example, a mentor exchange with you is near sacred and violating that trust would be rare. A coach and expert are professionals who also build their reputations guarding client information as confidential. Angels work to ethical guidelines that bind them not to discuss the business of one enterprise with another. After thoroughly qualifying a PathMaster, expect they can be trusted.

What About Confidentiality Agreements?

Generally, PathMasters are reluctant to sign secrecy, confidentiality, or non-disclosure agreements. They most likely will not sign because they constantly gain information from a wide range of business sources. They are ethically bound to keep separate what, and from whom they gained the information. Their professional value to you is the integrated knowledge of unidentified others applied to your problem.

Therefore, legally binding them not to divulge freely given company information is not in their professional best interest. They will not agree to keep all information you give them confidential but will agree to keep confidential all information you tell them you consider confidential.

How Much Access Should I Give PathMasters?

You set the physical and intellectual boundaries for PathMasters as they perform tasks. Here are some guidelines:

(1) Clarify the kinds of information PathMasters have and where they may get it.

(2) Good business practice is to use caution in disclosing unique business models, processes, formula, market data, scientific drawings, spreadsheet models and databases.

(3) Bad business practice is to disclose so little no one can understand the scope of your business problem.

(4) The mid-course is to relate enough information so the professional or listener understands your needs. Then, tell them how much you or your people do and do not know. Tell them where you have tried to find a right answer. You must tell the PathMaster enough to provide them with helpful and practical working guidelines. Agree on a plan and let them execute the task.

More About Sensitive Company Information

It is just good business to be careful with information you think is confidential. Telling too much or too little, where do you draw the line? Here is a practical approach.

Tell the PathMaster, *"I will be talking about information that I consider sensitive and it is very important that it not reach a competitor. I'm asking you not to discuss what we talk about with others."* Or, in an agreement to do the work insert the following:

> *Any drawings, reports, process diagrams, customer information, cost breakdowns, etc. is, and will remain, the property of the company. Further, that, (name _____) will not knowingly divulge or use for his private financial gain this information until such information is commonly known or made public by the company.*

Now the person is on notice and you have addressed ethical and moral standards.

Communicating - The Hardest Work of All

How you and a PathMaster understand what each other has said may be quite different. Not because one speaks a different language or speaks too fast or slow, I mean the "style" of how words are used. Mentors, coaches, experts, and angels have different listening and speaking styles. The same is true of you. No one is purposely trying to confuse or mislead the other. Each heard the others' words. However, here is the problem. We apply biasing filters to what we hear. So, the meaning of what was said and heard is different for each person. We choose to understand in a way to fit our purpose. Like a two-way radio, one end transmitted and the other end received. However, each end is not exactly tuned to the other's channel. Remember this saying, it is very helpful to explain verbal misunderstandings. **"I know you believe you heard what I said, but I am not sure you really understood what I meant to say."**

Speaking more precisely and slowly or loudly does help, but establishing unbiased listening and exact two-way channel settings results in honest understanding.

CHAPTER NINE

CARE AND FEEDING
OF A PATHMASTER

EXCITE PATHMASTERS WITH YOUR enthusiasm and commitment to your vision, plans, and people. Show them around your facility and have casual meetings with key people. Watch their behavior and listen to their questions. You must believe a PathMaster's experience and expertise will truly contribute to progress. Then, if it is right, explore working together.

O.K., you have decided to proceed. Be aware that PathMasters have at least two common characteristics. First, PathMasters must protect their reputations. They usually only accept engagements that will add to their reputation. Second, PathMasters want confirmation that you believe they are the best for great work to follow.

Your Communication Style with a PathMaster

Know what communication style to use when talking with a PathMaster.

> With a *Mentor* - be open, engaging, thoughtful, attentive, earnest, and honest.

> With a *Coach* - be inquisitive, engaged, descriptive, concerned, detailed, authoritative, decisive.

> With an *Expert* - be questioning, factual, deliberate, decisive.

> With an *Angel* - be factual, enthusiastic, urgent, honest, engaging, inviting.

PathMaster Communication Style With You:

> *Mentors* are cautious, reflecting, generalizing, unbiased, suggesting, involving, directive, constructively critical, measuring, and perhaps aloof.

> *Coaches* are inquisitive, friendly, excitable, expansive, focused, and urgent.

> *Experts* are superior, affected, professional, deliberate, measured, detailed, and aggressive.

> *Angels* are arrogant, probing, dubious, questioning, invasive, calculating, helpful, and formal.

The Chart below compares PathMaster styles.

PathMaster	Style	Skill	Rapport	Duration
Mentor	Open Impartial Reflective	Listening Illuminating Insightful	Close Deep Balancing	Several Years
Coach	Optimistic Enthusiastic Informal Biased	Training Teaching Showing Telling	Collegial Warm Interesting Collaborative	Months
Expert	Realistic Formal Judgmental	Searching Synthesizing Innovating	Imperious Confrontational Authoritative	Weeks
Angel	Careful Nervous Patient Formal	Probing Operating Intruding	Distant Cautious Demanding	Many Years

Is PathMaster Age Important?

A rule of thumb says there should be no more than 1½ generations between PathMaster and client. Your goal is to create the best fit between the PathMaster, you and your team.

Where Do I Find The Right PathMasters?

The **first task** is like going to the store. Make a list of what you need.

> ➤ What is the most critical problem I cannot fix?

> ➤ When do I want it fixed?

> ➤ When fixed, what will be the benefit?

> ➤ What are the qualifications of someone who can fix it?

> ➤ How much should I invest for such help?

The **second task** is to locate the right PathMaster. Start your search by sitting quietly and thinking about the following questions.

> ➤ Where does such a person work now?

> ➤ What specific experience is required to meet my needs?

> ➤ Which microenterprises, like mine, have worked with a PathMaster?

> ➤ Do I know someone in those companies I can contact for referrals for specific PathMasters?

> What task-related search keywords can I use to find useful business articles?

You are now prepared to contact business friends, or search the internet to collect names and contact information for possible PathMasters.

The **third task**, after identifying candidates, is to arrange a face-to-face meeting. A PathMaster's credentials are important but the right personal chemistries are more important. When meeting, start the qualification process by asking about their business background. Discuss how their career progressed by asking who, what, when and how long were typical client assignments. Now you can ask about specific task accomplishments.

> Does their experience match the situations you want to fix?

> Did they work for a microenterprise like yours?

> Ask about recent work they have completed.

Then request at least two reference names to contact about their work.

Culture Fit With My Company

Not all cultures and personality styles are the same. It is then most important that a PathMaster's business philosophy match your company's ethics and morals. The better the fit the more your team and the PathMaster will be able to communicate concepts, ideas, suggestions and training. During the interview listen for cultural, ethnic, or personal biases that could offend you or your team. Gauge whether their personal manner is acceptable, that is, not too aggressive or passive. Listen to their language and approach on how they would go about working on a problem. Then decide whether their style fits with your business style and practice.

For example, a coach should only offer training ideas and concepts that when heard by your team are similar to the ethics and principles of your enterprise. Experts installing a quality work program must have standards equal to your product or service quality goals. Although it is difficult to assess a perfect fit on first meeting, you will quickly detect a misfit.

A note about Americans. They have a lot to say about everything. They say it with directness using almost combative language. They are short on patience, particularly when people of other cultures do not immediately respond to or carry out their suggestions. Most other business cultures want to know how Americans achieve small enterprise success. As they learn about growing a business, they are usually uncomfortable by the manner in which Americans go about doing it.

Getting to the Details
You have decided that working with a PathMaster could be of help. Now let us better understand how they would get a fix on a problem, help with new initiatives

or train the team to be more efficient. Here are points to discuss:

> What you see as the problem; how or why it came about

> What ideas you and the team have about how the problem should be resolved

> What opinions or suggestions the PathMaster may have to fix the problem

> How the PathMaster proposes resolving the problem and how long would it take

> How much it will cost for the PathMaster to solve the problem

Paying the PathMaster

The old saying "you get what you pay for" applies here. Be careful accepting free help as its value is usually equal to what you pay – nothing.

Here is what happens. With the exception of Mentors, PathMasters prefer contracts or short agreements and work for a fee. Just arrive at a fair value after you both have clearly defined the tasks. Consider these elements:

> Look at the whole project and then determine the consulting time and materials costs needed to fix it.

> Agree on an hourly or daily consulting fee and specify all out-of-pocket expenses are to be billed at cost.

> Define project milestones, completion times and agree on progress payments.

Keep it simple, straightforward and professional. PathMasters are business people and are not on this earth to give you free help. Yes, you have an interesting story. Yes, we know times are difficult but here is the reality: you do not get something for nothing. Many PathMasters will freely spend their time to get acquainted. Their generosity, however, only lasts so long. When they transfer and receive their value, the agreed upon compensation must be paid.

Here are several ways to pay PathMasters. We all understand a cash payment. A trade or barter is the exchange of your goods or services equal in value to the agreed upon compensation. Another way is to pay a percentage of any increased sales or profit should their work lead to a new service, product development or market entry. A common substitute for cash, which is very difficult to calculate or agree upon, is an equivalent value of your company stock or percentage of enterprise ownership. Payment of some ownership of your enterprise is the least likely PathMaster compensation choice.

This chart details various PathMaster compensation options:

PathMaster	Cash	Barter	Commission	Stock	Payment Timetable
Mentor	Yes	Yes	No	Yes	Near Term
Coach	Yes	Yes	No	Maybe	Short Term
Expert	Yes	Yes	Maybe	Maybe	Short Term
Angels:					
Banker	Yes	No	Yes	Maybe	Medium Term
Private Party	No	Maybe	Maybe	Yes	Long Term
VC's	No	No	Maybe	Yes	Very Long
Lender	Yes	No	Yes	Maybe	Short Term
Family	Yes	Yes	Yes	Maybe	Short Term
Customer	No	Maybe	Yes	Yes	Medium

Dismissing the PathMasters with Care

Managing change to solve growth challenges evolves as a business grows. What worked before probably will not work now. A PathMaster who performed in the past may not now be as effective, relevant, or smart. You will get signals when it is time to change PathMasters. Their comments will now sound out of date. Proposed alternatives to fix problems do not really apply anymore. You will hear yourself say, "To tell you the truth, I'm not really sure why we spent so much time with this person." Or, "for that matter, I can't recall what was accomplished."

You are moving beyond the old to the new ways. It is what progress and growth mean. It is permissible to change helpers to move forward.

Perhaps during the assignment, the PathMaster simply did not perform well enough. Ending the assignment preserves internal company harmony, saves cash and time. However, do discharge a PathMaster with care. The decision takes thought, tact and diplomacy. The exit interview, while never pleasant, requires your skill to cleanly, and without resentment or hostility, end the arrangement. A simple reason is best. Afterwards, always advise whoever referred the PathMaster to you of your decision and action.

CHAPTER TEN

The Mentor

The Entrepreneurial Culture

A micropreneurial society's culture permits, encourages, and supports human energy and freedom to risk for the rewards of success. A passionate and dedicated individual or team can then convert a novel idea into a valued commercial reality. Talented people in all cultures want to and can grow an enterprise company around a personal or shared dream. What do successful micropreneurs say accounts for their confidence to pursue success? Some proceed by relying on their own skills, experience, and common sense. Many connect with a mentor who is an older and wiser micropreneur or seasoned manager. A mentor has been where you want to go. Whether you are a butcher, baker or candlestick maker, seek a mentor to increase your probability for business success.

The history of formal mentoring began when the more experienced first transferred practical knowledge to others. They were parents to children, brothers and sisters to each other, and anyone needing guidance. For example, the European cloth weaving Guild method of some 400 years ago coupled Master weavers to counsel, teach, encourage, and support a young apprentice in weaving craft competence. Two master-to-apprentice coupling models evolved. The first, an "arranged" method connects those with particular expertise and skill to those needing to acquire such knowledge and skill. Whether a trusting bond occurs is not important. The only goal is that learning take place.

The second model is a "random" connection. A chance meeting and/or introduction by a mutual friend starts the Master and apprentice relationship. Meetings, talks, and discussions may lead to a mentoring bond that carries forward into business help. The random model does not force a fit as a relationship may or may not evolve.

Today it is not practical to use either the arranged or the random process to find a mentor. Why? Busy micropreneurs simply cannot afford the time distraction to have one "assigned" or to rely on a "random" connection.

The new connecting model organizes mentoring. The goal is to quickly connect you to a mentor. To begin, you should understand the who, what, where, when and why about a mentor. The Mentor must understand your performance expectations and the skills you need from them.

To paraphrase what one writer, Daniel Levinson, said about mentors:

> "A Mentor can be of practical help to a younger person (entrepreneur) as they seek to find their way and gain new skills. But a good mentor is helpful in a more basic developmental sense. The relationship helps the recipient to identify with the person who exemplifies many of the qualities they seek. It enables them to form an internal figure that likes, admires, and encourages them in their struggles.

Levinson also noted mentors could be too young or too old. We may not regard the opinions, observations, or perspectives of people our own age or younger as credible. We may also easily discount or disregard what our peers say as they are usually telling us what they think we want hear, or have a competitor's bias. So, mentor counsel from peers may not be a good choice.

Similarly, engaging with people "too old" brings back feelings of how we listened to a parent. We "tuned out" or dismissed most of their observations, opinions and perspectives about our performance or behavior, labeling it "old school." We may even revert to our younger mindset when seriously discussing matters with someone our parent's age. For a younger person, the acceptable ethical and cultural norms of an older person may be at odds with today's standards. This can cause defensiveness or less objective listening. Changing these communication reactions are difficult no matter how mature we are.

WHAT IS A MENTOR

Upon hearing the word mentor, images of someone older, wiser and one who has much to share comes to mind. There is a special dynamic, a rapport, and relationship between the older mentor and the less experienced counsel seeker.

At some crucial point, a mentor probably helped you work through a difficult spot. "A mentor, I never had one!" says a strong, independent entrepreneur. Maybe nobody said, "I'd like you to meet a person called a mentor who has been over the path you are now walking." Nor did anyone say, "You know, what you need is a mentor. Why don't you ask around to see if you can find one?" My guess is that somehow you accidentally did connect to a mentor. You did not know why or how a rapport and friendship developed with that person. Perhaps a random meeting only occurred when it had to occur. What made it happen? Probably instant chemistry between both of you, some luck, perhaps an image or description that was in your mind. No matter, the time was right and a linkage made.

> *"Younger learners see their mentors as very successful, very knowledgeable, and very powerful, able to support and guide. Learners like, admire, respect, and look up to their mentors. A learner and mentor come to trust, take care of, and feel loyal to each other. Their relations become close, intimate, friendly, and perhaps affectionate."* – *Howell S. Baum, Ph.D. on mentors*

Did you just say to yourself, "I don't have time for what sounds like a deep emotional relationship?" "I have some business problems and just want sound advice. What's going on here?" Two business growth events are happening. A busy, new enterprise or a maturing micropreneur are converging. You and the business are now one. It is difficult to separate personal and business emotions, thinking processes and time commitments. This is when a mentor can help you sort out what is really important, reset focus and push for urgency. My job is to make you comfortable about finding and working with mentors as trusted confidants and experienced guides.

Let us go further. Why are Mentors different?

> ➤ If they were only a teacher, you would get instructions and be shown how.

> If they were only a counselor, you would present the problem and be given the answer.

> If they were only elders, you would sit at their knee, receive wisdom and follow their advice.

Entrepreneurs only grow by making their own decisions. They assess facts, decide what is urgent, and measure the resources available. You cannot grow by only doing what a teacher, counselor, or elder says to do. A mentor's value is to make you engage with challenges and to talk about possible alternative solutions. A mentor does not judge, tell, preach, lecture, or do. No other PathMaster relationship generates the same level of trust as the one that grows between you and a mentor.

WHERE TO FIND A MENTOR

Mentors are preferably eight and no more than 20 years older than you are. They are experienced and busy. They are not among your friends or your parent's circle of friends. Business association members are a good source. Maybe someone that works for a supplier or customer. Perhaps the person you met on a plane trip that will exchange ideas via email. They are around. Just be open to meeting one.

One good way to find a mentor is to seek counsel from owners or managers of businesses similar to yours. Make a list of those some distance away from your trading area and contact the owner by email or phone. Ask how long they have been in the product, retail, or service business. Tell them you are struggling with some business problems, that you are not a direct competitor and would like to talk about how they overcame some obstacles. Most probably, you will learn the owner has met and solved most of the challenges you now face. You really do not compete because of distance separation. These contacts are excellent mentor candidates.

Other referral sources are attorneys/solicitors, bankers or accountants. Tell them you need an experienced listener who can be trusted and wants to share and help someone who has an exciting small business "vision." Follow up every referral. Offer to meet the potential mentor whenever and wherever is convenient.

GETTING A MENTOR ENGAGED TO HELP

Assume your hunt was a success and a first meeting is to take place. While you are gauging the mentor, the mentor will be gauging you. Here is what you are looking for:

You want to know if the mentor:

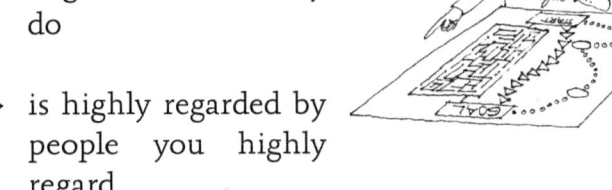

> is good at what they do

> is highly regarded by people you highly regard

> has a good community reputation

- has a good discussion style

- motivates you

- seems self-confidant

- meets your goal expectations and budget

The mentor wants to know about your:

- intelligence

- ambitions

- need and ability to accept responsibility

- loyalty commitments

- work and managing style

- organizing know-how

- attitudes about success

- family and relaxation priorities

While talking, sense if the chemistry feels good. Then show him around your facilities and introduce him to your key people. Explain your vision and ask whether he would consider exchanging ideas with you as a trusted advisor.

Even though the interview went well, do not settle on the first mentor you meet. He or she is only the right person by making comparisons to other candidates. Involvement with a mentor is not a trivial decision. Take the time to find someone who fits you.

WORKING WITH A MENTOR

Business journals, blogs, and websites report mentoring as an effective way to help younger workers advance their careers in large corporate environments. They describe a mentor as a coach, a political advocate, and protector of a younger businessperson. The work and people dynamics are different for large and small companies. Big company mentoring models do not work for a small enterprise. Entrepreneurs are looking for mentors who are objective, listen, and then set up a path to follow.

TALKING WITH A MENTOR

Discussing issues with a mentor is quite different than talking with any other outside helper. Conversation characteristics of a mentor are:

> ➤ dialogue is open, probing, with much give and take

> ➤ listening is quiet and intent

> discussion is objective, synthesizing, logical and prioritized, constructive

> proposing is reflective, illuminating, non-judgmental and suggestive

> overall no lectures, no solutions, no pat answers

Trust develops when there is openness and honesty between you and a mentor. When this happens, you will be eager to share business concerns. When answering the mentor's questions there are information boundaries to observe. Do be careful with private company information; however, the more you are willing to share, the more the mentor can better serve you.

A GOOD MENTOR ASKS A SERIES OF EASY QUESTIONS ABOUT AN ISSUE. WITHOUT KNOWING IT, YOUR ANSWERS LEAD THINKING TO A PRACTICAL CONCLUSION. THE MENTOR HEARS ALL YOU SAID AND FORMS A BEST OBSERVATON AND CONCLUSION. THEN LETS YOU MAKE A DECISION.

Set information boundaries with the mentor and your company team:

➤ instruct everyone to help the mentor.

➤ ask the team to check with you about unusual mentor information requests.

➤ be cautious of them roaming the office, store or facility areas, as team members may see the mentor as your spy, or as only gathering opinions for your review.

➤ inform the team to tell the mentor only information you have approved, such as sales figures, product or service costs, certain spreadsheets, software code or key customers.

➤ be patient when mentors ask about matters you feel are not "on the subject." Remember, they may be assembling perspectives and alternatives you have not considered. Regard a mentor as the most friendly of all PathMasters.

HOW TO COMPENSATE A MENTOR

Good business rules are: "you cannot get something for nothing!" and "for value received, equal value must be paid." So, to the PathMasters who help, your moral obligation is a fair compensation. They are suppliers of know-how, information and practical counsel. Consider these mentor compensation methods:

1. A monthly cash amount made available when promised. This flat rate includes many or few hours of work. Such an agreement to work together tells the mentor that you truly want his counsel.

2. Give the mentor a future opportunity, called an option, to invest in your business. This is how it works. The mentor does not take cash for services provided but a credit for an equal amount toward purchasing a percent of company ownership or increased profit. This method communicates your belief the mentor's counsel will increase the business value.

3. Stock and cash to equal the value you and the mentor agree is fair.

4. A cash payment to the mentor based upon an agreed money rate for time spent or task completed.

TIME FOR THE MENTOR TO GO

As the business grows, you may outgrow the mentor. It is time to depart the formal arrangement. The event should occur when you believe their services are no longer helpful. Reasons to disengage may be an unsatisfactory personal style or the business has just evolved beyond their mentoring skills.

Examples of negative Mentor styles:

> too pedantic, preaching, opinionated, commanding, judgmental

> too accommodating, or rigid, unyielding, and inattentive

> thinks ahead of the discussion point to have a quick reply

> engages in team politics; is too talkative and demanding of your time

Examples of negative Mentor skills:

> not focused on your concerns

> not experienced enough to offer reasonable alternatives

> not professional enough to command credibility and the respect of your team

> not confidential enough with information about your business

> not quick enough to keep up with your thinking

No single mentor weakness is reason to dismiss a mentor. However, repeated negative behavior or skill weakness warns of needed change. When it is time to say goodbye, consider these comments:

"The business is entering a new phase and you have helped us get here. Now I think it is best to find someone else who has been where we are going." Let the mentor express his anger, agreement, hurt, rejection or, probably relief.

Then you can say, "Good, I hope we can ask for your counsel from time to time. Thank you."

Or try another approach, "This is hard for me. You have really been my strong support. You helped me over many barriers during this phase of our growth. Your background was a perfect fit up to now, but the new issues I may confront could be greater than your experience. It is time for us to decide whether you can still provide what we need. I value our relationship and know we will be talking often. However, the formal assignment must end."

One more way could go like this, "I thought we would be able to develop a positive working style to help me and satisfy you. I do not feel that has or can happen. So, it is best that we conclude the relationship now before problems really occur. I sincerely appreciate your effort and time trying to make this work, but it did not. Let us keep in contact."

You can vary these themes but always let the mentor leave without losing face, understanding your reasons to close the engagement, and feeling comfortable they contributed.

CHAPTER ELEVEN

THE COACH

PROFILING A COACH

The Coach is outgoing, confidant and focused to do the job. Their business is to teach, show, organize, and motivate people to change the way they do things. As in sports, a coach strengthens and builds muscles, shows how to make the right moves, and drills on running plays causing each player to depend or each other in order to build team spirit.

This PathMaster is delightful. His manner and training methods are crisp and matter-of-fact. Enjoy the relationship.

FINDING A COACH

This PathMaster is easy to locate. Here are ideas about where to look for a coach.

- microenterprise coaching/training service firms or respected business people

- other micropreneurs or small enterprise manager referrals

- directories and web references for microbusiness coaching professionals

QUALIFYING A COACH

A coach persuades people into action. As teachers, they change people's minds. Be cautious. Confirm their track record to prove they can do the job. Coaches should not be more than 10 years older than the enterprise team they will work with.

Here is a suggested hiring process:

- evaluate if their credentials meet your needs and ask for references.

- meet the Coach to hear their experience and "test" the personal chemistry.

- start the interview with a "get to know you" talk about your company.

- describe the coaching challenge as you see it.

- define the training tasks and goals then outline the results you expect.

- now, let the coach talk about his strategy to meet the challenges.

- ask and discuss what coaching methods and processes are best used.

- evaluate the coach's sense of urgency. Do the ideas meet your needs?

- discuss tasks, timetables, next steps and compensation.

- end the interview and thank the Coach for coming to your office.

Then ask your team to answer "yes or no" to these questions.
Did the Coach:

- identify the reasons why your operations are not working?

- just restate your thoughts?

- directly answer questions?

- accept your timetables? If no, ask why.

- dress, think and speak well when coaching your team?

> show a video or slideshow of their training style?

Now, discuss with them and agree whether to accept or reject the Coach candidate.

Coach Qualifies You and the Team

The candidate will also rate your people. Here is what they ask themselves:

> Did the micropreneur signal I could add value to the enterprise?

> Did they identify and accept core issues needing attention?

> Did they seem comfortable with the training cost?

> Did they have realistic expectations about task timetables?

> Did they agree some coaching tasks need new tools?

The company and candidate decide to go forward and meet to formalize the objectives and tasks, work processes, time for start and completion, company information agreements, and compensation arrangements. Hiring a coach is an easy investment decision by answering the following question: "Am I able to develop the needed experience internally, as fast as I can accomplish results using someone from outside?"

WORKING WITH A COACH

Coaching means action that transfers know-how to others who then fix the problem. The Coach listens and surveys your needs. They propose training, showing, or telling solutions. They define tasks, measurable results and timetables. The Coach does the job and leaves.

TALKING WITH A COACH

A Coach needs certain information to prepare effective training sessions. Examples of information a coach may need:

> team data of salaries, resumes, work reviews

> sales data - new versus old customers, competition, product test data

> production data - inventory turnover, shipping history, cost breakdowns

> R&D - 1st user test results, patent coverage, competitor comparisons

> operations - annual budget, financial statements, written company policies

> financial data - unit price and cost breakdowns, expense analysis

Give the coach enough detail to create and develop new methods and approaches to show and train your people. Retain all company documents used or created by the coach.

HOW TO COMPENSATE A COACH

There are several fee options that a coach will accept: cash paid on an hourly, daily or fixed-fee basis; a royalty or commission percentage of measurable improvement of company business, due to their training or advice; rarely stock in lieu of cash; barter for a like value; a combination of some cash and other means to equal their fee. The coach usually prefers a simple cash arrangement.

CAUTIONS ABOUT WORKING WITH A COACH

Your team will learn more from a comfortable coaching style. After watching a few sessions, you can judge if a coach is being effective by:

> how they dress and present themselves, the way they talk, the words they use, clarity and training session props and tools.

> how they guide work completion timetables, mix training and work sessions, get the team participating.

> how they show the team practical and usable methods.

Your team will learn less from an unprofessional coach who is:

> not prepared to start work at the agreed time.

> not sensing if the trainee is learning.

> not matching training tools to your business and team vocabulary.

> not meeting the coaching project milestones.

> not building greater teamwork among employees.

> not advising you about progress, problems or suggesting coaching goal changes.

Remember, you hired a coach that claimed professionalism and experience. You both agreed on the task work and completion timetables. If the Coach is not performing and not accepting your corrective suggestions, give the Coach one more chance. If your directions to the Coach are still not accepted, then get somebody else.

ENDING THE ENGAGEMENT

The separation is businesslike. Here are typical "good-bye" phrases. For a job well done you could say, "Well, your work is finished. We gained much and you executed the project well. I will be happy to recommend your services to anyone. I am sure we will call you again."

OR, for a job not well done - "I thought, as you did, there was a good fit with your experience and our company problems. We were wrong. You and I are at fault for not taking the time to assure the fit. So I now must end the engagement. Thank you for your time. I will make sure your fee is paid promptly."

CHAPTER TWELVE

THE EXPERT

WHAT IS AN EXPERT

An Expert has the answer, but just does NOT know the question! They have special knowledge of narrow market niches, manufacturing and cost reduction methods, where to apply technologies, financial efficiencies, and personnel issues.

Like the Coach, the expert sells information and their career experiences. The expert is self-confidant, open and responsive and has a strong opinion about subjects of their particular field. They are direct, challenging and will change your opinions of business

reality. They are a very interesting, stimulating, and exciting PathMaster.

Finding an Expert

Experts are easy to find. Here is where to look for one:

> authors of professional journals or industry publication articles

> analysts of government or industry studies

> subject specialists working for a market leader or supplier, or trade association

> researchers from a university or corporate laboratory

> owners of a business just like yours in non-competitive geography

> references from web searches using domain subject keywords

The expert's age is important because it relates to their domain knowledge. Here are a few age-related selection guidelines.

> retail and old economy service businesses: minimum age is 40

> technology or science fields: minimum age is 32, and maximum age is 55

> product development, light production, marketing and financial: minimum age is 35, and maximum age is 55

PREPARING TO WORK WITH THE EXPERT

Can you find the answers yourself? Sure! Your toughest job when searching for accurate answers is first finding the most important questions. To do this you must objectively and fearlessly ask, "What is the information I need to move the business forward." Identify this key information before meeting the Expert.

Your business records will give you clues to new information needed. Here is where to look:

> bookkeeping records to identify major cost and sales trends

> product and service sales numbers and details of customer returns

> causes of missed goals for new items, projects or programs

> cost estimates compared to final cost of producing, servicing or selling

> purchasing records to determine if costs are going up or down

> average sales per employee, per day, per meal served, per retail transaction

> worker hourly or annual salary rate records to make competitive comparisons

Decide whether you or others are able to uncover important answers. If your decision is we cannot, be ready with questions when the expert arrives.

The goal of the interview is to feel confident the expert will find and clearly deliver the answers you seek. Keep talking until you and the expert understand the plan to obtain the information you need.

After telling Experts what your key questions are, here are questions for them:

> "Tell me about your background."

> "Describe other work where you found answers for questions similar to ours."

> "You heard our questions, how would you go about getting us answers?"

> "Do you search for and collect the answers, or use existing data from others?"

> "Do you prefer delivering such answers in a written report or by talking?"

> "When are you available to start?"

> "May we contact others to discuss your previous work?"

Establishing the Assignment

Be clear and precise with an expert. Ask for a work proposal that:

> details the information needed

> describes work methods and specifies outcomes

> defines project start and finish times

> specifies terms of compensation for work completed

WORKING WITH AN EXPERT

They are careful listeners. They ask questions starting with who, why, what, when, how many and how much. **[See Appendix One for "Questions They Ask,"** a qualified expert will ask many of these]. The expert should guide the discussion to build a ranked set of questions needing answers. You and the expert agree on proposed methods to collect the information. They go off to do the work, interpret and analyze answers, deliver and discuss their report and leave.

TALKING WITH AN EXPERT

Experts deeply probe all issues because you and your team are often reluctant to admit what you do not know. These questions are threatening and uncomfortable for all. However, when the expert knows what you do not know, their work can begin.

Do not worry too much about confidentiality because an expert brings more information into the enterprise than they could possibly carry out. If you are concerned about certain private papers or documents, it is appropriate to request the Expert to sign a non-disclosure agreement.

BENEFITS OF WORKING WITH AN EXPERT

Maybe "you are too close to the forest to see the trees." The expert quickly illuminates the hidden or missing information you could not see. They link outside reality to inside problems. Sometimes an expert's sharp focus and their lens of objective reality will impress you. As new information is gathered, you can use an expert to quickly and objectively strengthen your strategy and plans.

MANAGING THE EXPERT

You need information help. You know the expert can get it. The expert responds best to directness. At project outset, tell them:

- ➤ you want progress reports

- ➤ early warnings of problems they are having

> whether you can assist the effort in any way

> you will study and be prepared to discuss their report findings

The expert will ask for confirmation that you know their work results are without bias and will only reflect "real world" opinions based on facts. Once reported, they will not change their results to match your perception of the world.

HOW TO COMPENSATE THE EXPERT

Here are normal fee options for Experts:

> cash for time spent or a fixed project fee. Most experts prefer fixed price assignments.

> royalty or commission for identifying a new market, referring new customers to your enterprise or shop, locating lower cost suppliers, arranging a technology or product line sale or purchase or initiating a marketing partnership. The expert rarely asks for your company stock as payment.

Make fee arrangements at the beginning of the project to avoid potential misunderstandings. Negotiate tough-mindedly but fairly with experts.

Here are final comments about the cost and value of the Expert. Your time is more valuable than an expert's time. Your time investment is to form the right questions.

Your investment in their time to locate the information, perform unbiased evaluations, and reach problem-solving conclusions is a good value.

DISENGAGING FROM AN EXPERT

Experts operate in a precise manner. You may find they do not fit when:

> ➤ they are too narrowly or broadly defining information needs and you conclude the results will not be useful

> ➤ they are too experienced or inexperienced for the information needed

> ➤ they are too fast or slow in completing the work

> ➤ the results were not original work but taken from published sources

Disengage from this PathMaster, as with a Coach, in a clean and business-like manner.

CHAPTER THIRTEEN

THE ANGELS

YOUR ENTERPRISE NEEDS CAPITAL to grow beyond its micro start-up stage. The business is growing because of human capital work by you and your team, emotional capital spent by your family, trusting capital offered by customers and suppliers, and money capital provided by believers in your vision. Each will risk for a different reason. They all trust to gain reward. Securing capital is vital to the survival and growth of the enterprise. The Angel investor is the one you must seek and convince that your enterprise has reward potential.

Raising capital is the hardest task you will face. It is frustrating, tiring, emotional, discouraging, and constant work. At times, you will not care who invests and just say, "give me the money." But, be careful. It is as risky for you to take money from any Angel and just as risky for Angels to invest in just anyone. You and an Angel will live a long time together so each other's goals must be compatible.

WHAT IS AN ANGEL

Angels come in differ-
ent shapes and forms from
many places. All are similar
but risk capital investment
for different reasons under
different repayment terms.
Let us meet them.

Bankers focus on risk.
They loan money accord-
ing to financial rules secured by pledges of your
tangible assets. They lend using your hard assets, ac-
tual revenue and profit to repay a loan. They have limited skill or interest in judging the accuracy of your
forecasts. They do not make lending decisions on your
faith or hope but on their judgment of your potential
for success.

Wealthy individuals invest in higher risk ventures expecting a higher reward than a loan. They are less interested in your business numbers or assets. However,
they must understand your vision and business plan
coupled with your passion to succeed. This money is
not available for proprietorships. Capital is available
after the microventure has shown continuing sales by
a dedicated team and has become a corporation with
shares to sell.

Professional venture capitalists (VCs) mostly invest in corporations, not proprietorships or partnerships. They consider investing in an enterprise and team that has survived beyond the feasibility or "proof-of-concept" micro stage, usually 3-4 years after start-up and after achieving sales to sustain the enterprise. VCs exchange the value of their cash for stock ownership value in your company. They are capable and qualified to evaluate the current and potential value of your company. They aggressively barter to minimize their risk and maximize a future reward. They have a strong influence on how enterprise management seeks and achieves a positive cash flow, satisfies customers, and turns a profit. For VC's, microventure investment risk is far greater than any perceived rewards. [See **Appendix Two** – "**All about venture capitalists**"]

Suppliers and customers invest by allowing you time to pay for goods or services purchased, or by paying you cash when they order your goods or services. These investments improve your cash flow. They usually do not invest capital for company ownership or make loans.

Family and friends buy your company stock or loan you money because of their personal ties to you or someone on your team. They seldom ask many questions about financials or business plans. They want to help your vision succeed. Family and friends are, in the long term, the least desirable potential investors.

More Angels

Two additional angels can provide capital or improve cash flow. They are (1) government agencies that issue grants and contracts for work to use the skills or expertise within the enterprise, and (2) non-bank loan companies that lend money to high credit risk firms at high interest rates.

Angel Investors

During your capital courtship with Angels, there is much activity. There are meetings, presentations, email exchanges and negotiations about the future value of the business. All this ends with an investor saying, "Yes, we will" or "No, not at this time."

After the transaction of Angel money for an equal value ownership in your company, expect activities like this between Angels and the microenterprise:

> ➤ Angels expect you and the corporation's Board of Directors wisely use the company resources to increase profit and thus the value of company stock shares.

> ➤ Angels do not want day-to-day operations reports.

> ➤ Angels like to attend major company events. It is good for team morale, community relations and reinforces the Angel's investment judgment.

➤ You work hard to complete the business plan tasks, to meet timetables, and to produce sales and profits. The Angel works to monitor company progress and management commitments.

➤ Angels expect you to spend their money as if it came from your own pocket.

When your business is young and money is low, it is tempting to agree to whatever the suggested terms are. You need the money today and cannot worry about tomorrow. Your thoughts are any arrangement made now can be changed later. Be careful. Quickly agreeing to conditions that "mortgage your future" can delay company growth.

FINDING AN ANGEL

Investor money is plentiful. Investing opportunities are scarce. Search for investors in your local area, region or country, within local or national business newspaper and magazine articles or banking directories. Ask for referrals from entrepreneurs of firms your size that has

secured risk capital. Talk with attendees at microenterprise meetings. Create introductions to wealthy people in your community or country, particularly successful micropreneurs. Knock on your neighbor's door. An Angel may open it.

HIRING an ANGEL

Angels are not for hire. Only they decide whether they will work with you!

WORKING WITH ANGELS

The number one priority is to develop a micro business plan for discussion with Angels. Money wants to hear and see you tell them your plan, whether simple or very detailed. There are easy to use, step-by-step models available on the internet for developing your own plan. Take your unique enterprise and mold the internet plan around your own facts and goals. You must take many hours to think through each risk reduction milestone with timetables to attain success goals. These include customer definitions and product or service value you will offer at what price and at what cost. Investors need only have <u>reasonable assumptions</u> of the future as the future has no facts. Insisting on seeing your plan is the investor's method to force you to take the journey from where you are to where you want to go. The plan itself is less important to the investor than your conviction in telling them about the journey.

The Bankers - How they Work

Bankers have rather rigid loan rules and guidelines. They lend amounts up to 60% of tangible assets that are easily convertible into cash. Their reward is interest collected at percentage rates greater than rates they pay bank customers on savings accounts.

Your Advantage

> ➤ loaned money does not buy company ownership

> ➤ the transaction time is fast

> ➤ involvement in your business is minimal

Your only disadvantage is the loan repayment must be timely no matter what negative or sudden situation occurs.

Bank financing is a good choice for micro or very early stage enterprises if you agree to pledge personal assets. After meeting payment schedules, a bank will loan with just a personal agreement that you will make good on the loan. As the business grows, bank loans are best to fund building inventory and operating cash, while purchasing equipment, expanding facilities or waiting for customers to pay your invoices.

Private Investors

These wealthy individuals commit a small portion of their total investing portfolio to purchase small, private company stock. They take such risk for high potential returns. These Angels often become passionate about your vision. They are less skilled and demanding than a VC when evaluating an investing proposal and offer you less company-building experience than potential advisors.

Private investor capital allows a very small company to develop, launch and confirm market acceptance of a product or service. Again, venture capitalists rarely invest in this early company life stage.

Your Advantage

> - cash for company stock

> - modest information needed to invest

> - long-term investors for five or more years

Your Disadvantage:

> - prohibits pay back of any loans you have made to the company

> - limited capital for your future needs

> - may want periodic dividends or interest plus stock

This Angel expects a reward of three to five times the amount they invest. They are prepared to lose all principal should the company fail. It is good practice to have a private investor confirm their financial ability to accept such risk.

Government Angels

National, state, and local government agencies make contracts with and grants to microenterprises to develop and enter markets or develop technology. You are only required to submit progress reports to reach the grant or contract goals.

Government Angel goals are to create new jobs, advance local industry, establish and grow new retail or service outlets, prove new science or technology feasibility leading to products or services, and to increase domestic or export revenue. It is not charity. Rather, it is a method to stimulate local, regional and national employment or local growth.

Your Advantage

> ➤ capital that does not reduce your ownership

> ➤ capital you must repay only with work

Your Disadvantage

> ➤ a grant or contract takes time and is difficult

> work schedules are fixed and periodic reporting may be complex

> inventions that are patent protected and developed using these funds may be used by anyone

The reason the public can use patents developed under government grants is simple to explain. Citizens pay taxes to governments. Public agencies use taxes to make grants or give contracts. The public has some right to what their money helped to develop. Public money puts you to work. Your company develops something novel and worth seeking a patent. You pursue that novelty and are first in the market. Your company has an advantage until the patent becomes valid and published. After the patent issues, the government and its contractors can use what the patent teaches.

There is no need to be concerned about this situation. Look at it this way. A competitor needs about one year to test and develop a novel idea for commercial feasibility. Making it market ready takes another year. During these two years, while the competitor prepares, you are selling in the market. In the third year, you have developed and are selling new features when the patent is issued and available to the public.

So, for two years you will be selling to customers. Do not worry about the future public use of your patent. Focus on finding and developing new ways to invent around your issued patent. If you do not, somebody else will.

Patents and Copyrights

The saying goes, "a patent just gives its owner the right to go to court to defend it." However, a protected new method or process of doing something better, or composition of unique materials, or a clothing design, manuscript or software code, photo or design, product or service brand name or logo has value. Legally protect these enterprise assets by a patent, copyright or trademark.

After protecting your idea the patent or license

> ➤ may be sold for cash

> ➤ used as a bartering tool to create business alliances

> ➤ become a barrier to others to defend your market positions

Make a plan to bring the novel idea to proof-of-concept or commercial feasibility. Only seek protection of those potential innovations that will significantly improve performance or efficiency over what the customer is presently using. Small incremental performance increases are not worth the protection costs. Allow an expert or patent counsel to determine the idea's potential commercial value.

The Least Desirable Angels - Family Members and Friends

"How exciting!" they say, "You are going to start a new enterprise?" Or, "Saw your business door is open." They then say, "If you need financial help with a loan or if I can maybe invest in your enterprise, please let me know!" This may sound familiar and inviting. You then consider asking them for help. Be careful, these are risky waters.

These Angels are the easiest sources to approach for money. That is the good news. But the bad news is there may be future sad feelings. Some cultures discourage business dealings with family or personal friends. Whether your culture thinks it is right or wrong, do consider family and friends as possible Angels. Again, be very careful.

Your Advantage taking money from these Angels

> they make interest-bearing loans or want some ownership of your enterprise

> their decision to give you money is emotional - they know you

> there is minimum if any involvement in the business

Your Disadvantage

> they are naive when assessing business risks

- unlike private investors, they cannot afford to lose money

- they always want their money back

- they react emotionally when not repaid causing friction, doubts, and separation between you and family members or friends

- they will react by being angry or feel you have betrayed their trust

- your family and friends become less important to you than the business

Taking their money is VERY DANGEROUS. COMPANY FAILURE CAN DESTROY RELATIONSHIPS. Ask family or friends for capital only in extremely desperate company times.

Commercial Loan Companies and Credit Unions

This Angel's repayment terms are stricter than a bank. This means higher interest rates on loans and less patience with late payments. When a loan becomes "troubled," they stop new loans to you. They may demand all money be repaid and will take any steps to get their capital back - another dangerous money source.

Meeting With Angels

It is best to invite an Angel to come to your premises and meet your team. Here are steps to prepare for the meeting.

Organizing the Meeting

Telephone, email or write the Angel to introduce yourself. Tell them what your business does and what you want to do. Briefly describe whether the business plan is on track. Suggest meeting at your office, store or home. Offer to send a business plan summary or any details they may request. Bankers usually ask for a complete business plan before they visit. Resist their request by saying, "Parts of our plan need final adjustment. I would appreciate your views on the plan's strengths and weaknesses you feel need special discussion when we meet." Sometimes this approach works. So, if you have not prepared a well-reasoned business plan, DO IT NOW.

Send an agenda for the proposed meeting and information about you and your management. Gain their acceptance to meet. Call to confirm a day before.

There are housekeeping chores before the meeting:

> Make work areas appear well organized

> Tidy up - hide coffee cups, sandwich bags, and clear desks or counters

> Instruct your team to "look busy"

> Ensure equipment is working, lighting is bright, all are wearing clean clothes

> The meeting area is free of clutter, store floor, counters and display cases clean

> Work diagrams, product photos, or testimonial letters are available

> Pre-check electronic projection equipment and clean all writing surfaces

> Have water, soft drinks and coffee available

> NO phone calls or texting when meeting with an Angel

> Money is serious business - be dressed for success

The Meeting

You must control the meeting. Follow an agenda with these elements:

> Date, time, place, people present and their affiliation

> Company background and status

> Support of product or service uniqueness claims

> Profile of customers and orders filled with competitive comparisons

> Tour of facility and discussion of the near term sales outlook

> Discuss forecast assumptions for revenue, profit and loss, and cash flow

> Meeting summary and any additional information needed to proceed

> Next steps and future meeting time

Angels want and should get your financial information and company forecasts. They need facts and validated assumptions to make investment decisions. Let them meet your team so they can see who will carry out the plans. Be engaging, cooperative and free with your time. Convince them of your passion and energy to accomplish the company plan. Invite them to visit and discuss milestone progress. Angels do not need all, but just enough, information to gain confidence that their future rewards are greater than the near term investment or loan risk.

Follow-up

The meeting is over. Now make sure the Angel is enthusiastic. Confirm that each of you has genuine interest to proceed. Do not be timid. Call them a few days after you deliver the additional requested information. They hear many business stories. You are competing with many others seeking capital.

During the second or third follow-up call, ask why the process is not moving faster. You might question, "Do you see any barriers to an investment or loan?" A hard question because you may not want to hear the answer. Ask it anyway. Your team is depending on you to obtain the needed capital. YOU NEED NOT BE GOOD FRIENDS WITH AN ANGEL ONLY A DESIRE FROM EACH FOR A RESPECTFUL WORKING ALLIANCE.

Evaluating an Angel

Angels bring more value to your table than money. They can only contribute when you have allowed them to understand your thinking about the enterprise's future. You cannot evaluate money, as money is money. You can, however, evaluate the Angel's experience and judge how much non-financial value they may add.

Angels supply or withhold money based on your results. Meeting milestones and goals usually assure continued funding. Falling behind does not work, no matter the reason. Whatever is happening, continually review, evaluate and manage your Angel relationship. Determine whether you both:

> ➤ are clearly understanding the other

- are answering information requests promptly

- are more positive or more negative when you meet

- are helping to get new business for the company

- are fault-finding or cooperating

- are deeply enthusiastic about a shared company vision

- are fair minded of the other's viewpoints

- are forming ties to meet future problems

- are open enough to challenge each other's opinion

Bankers and Commercial loan companies want to review:

- profit and loss statements for the past 3 to 5 years

- checking and savings account balances, value of company assets, trade receivables and payables, product or service brochures, place of business photos and the enterprise's internet addresses

- who are major customers and suppliers

- who owns more than 5% of the company stock

- personal financial statements of management members owning more than 20% of the company stock including detail of assets like a house, car, vacation home, etc.

- a detailed future 18 month operating budget of revenue, costs, marketing and administrative expenses and cash flow projection

When meeting with bank and commercial loan company Angels, describe your plan, answering all questions they may ask. Their job is to listen, then later verify what they heard, read and saw. So be helpful, instructive and wait to answer their next question.

HOW TO COMPENSATE THE ANGEL

Simple, they expect to get all the money they invested or loaned returned with a profit. Different Angels have different return expectations.

Private Angel Investors

Private investors will usually agree to a loan at better terms than a bank. They also agree to purchase company stock at a price greater than paid by a venture capitalist. For example, the company offers its stock for a price of 100. Private investors may agree to a stock price at a value of 80. VC's will negotiate the price down further to 70. An investor reality is the lower of the initial price paid for your stock the higher their future return. Your goal is to sell the least number of shares at the highest price to get the money you need.

Private investors like to be financial partners in very young enterprises. They will wait while you grow, sometimes as long as 10 years. They are anticipating a return of 20 to 30 times what they invested for taking an early risk and being patient.

Banker Angels

Reward for taking a risk is the loan interest you return to them. Bankers ask that you pay an interest rate 3 to 5% higher than they earn from loans for homes, from borrowers with something real to pledge against the loan, or from the interest they pay on savings accounts.

Bankers study your cash-flow forecasts, challenge your revenue assumptions, and then decide the loan terms. They demand timely interest and principal payments. This Angel may also want more than just a cash interest return. They may request a future right, called a warrant or option, to buy the company stock at a price equal to the company value at the time of the loan. A banker may ask for this loan condition but you must fight hard to reject this request. To agree will reduce your ownership.

The banker usually asks if you are the sole or majority business owner. Next, they will ask whether you will pledge some personal asset to assure loan repayment. This loan term is an important family matter needing very careful consideration. These terms and conditions often make bank borrowing expensive.

REMEMBER THIS ABOUT A PRIVATE INVESTOR, BANKER, AND VC ANGELS: THEY DO NOT WANT TO OWN MORE THAN 50 PERCENT OF YOUR ENTERPRISE BECAUSE THEY THEN MUST RUN IT. ALSO, IF YOU AND YOUR TEAM ARE LESS THAN 50% OWNERS YOUR PASSION AND ENERGY TO SUCCEED WILL BE GREATLY LESSENED.

Government Angel Grants and Contracts
The government only wants timely reports and prudent execution of a grant or contract.

Family & Friends
Receiving capital from this source is the easiest, fastest and potentially least intrusive approach. They expect the loan to yield the current interest rate. They want to buy your company stock at a reasonable value.

Suppliers/Vendors and Customers/Buyers
These angels are an excellent capital source for an early commercial enterprise. Here is how suppliers and customers invest:

> ➤ suppliers often allow invoice payment up to 90 to 120 days for goods and services they sell to the enterprise; therefore you are receiving a loan from the supplier.

> ➤ customers make a prepayment of 25 to 50% of the

total purchase value when placing their order, which usually covers the cost of goods or services.

> suppliers may expect interest payments on delayed payment balances. They may also request a fraction of the delayed payment amount in equal value of enterprise stock, warrants or an option to buy the enterprise stock at the price paid by the last investor.

These investment methods increase company cash flow and are far superior to bank loans or direct equity investment. With this Angel, you only have one chance. You must execute perfectly to the terms and conditions required by suppliers. When you perform, then trust develops. A weakened trust may damage this financing relationship.

Why will suppliers or customers accept this risk? The answer is competition. They want new, unique and cost-reducing products and services as ways to reach their end user customers. Often a new enterprise lacks adequate capital to begin reaching the market. If the new company fails to sell new products or services, the competitive marketplace remains the same. Aggressive suppliers use the non-out-of-pocket mechanisms to finance a new market competitor.

Is the risk of using suppliers and customers worth the reward? Yes, it is. TAKE THE MONEY, but build and maintain their trust. Make sure payments and deliveries are either early or always on time.

Commercial Loan and Credit Union Companies

Loan company managers are good at what they do but have limited experience or feel for what it takes to grow a small enterprise. They focus on risk reducing collateral to secure the loan. Sad stories about your business are of no interest to them. They just want their money. So this angel is a less desirable capital source.

They loan money within these limits and terms:

➤ 60 to 70% of what customers owe the company

➤ 40 to 50% of resale value of the enterprise's fixed assets, e.g.: furniture, machines, trucks and automobiles

➤ 50 to 60% of the loan amount from a lien on the owner or team member's financial assets. It is rare that team members will agree to such loan conditions as they are not significant enterprise owners nor are they deciding on financial business matters.

➤ 60% of the loan amount co-signed or secured by a third party's assets

> offer little margin for late payment

> secure their loaned capital by selling pledged collateral

General Angel Expectations

ANGELS	INVESTMENT	TIME	RETURN
Bankers	Medium	Medium	Average
Private Investors	Low	Long	High
Venture Capital	High	Very Long	Very High
Buyers/Vendors	Very Low	Short	Very Low
Family/Friends	Very Low	Longer	Average

DISENGAGING FROM AN ANGEL

Angel money arrangements work well for the most part, but sometimes they do not. Angels are committed investors in your future. They must help until the enterprise repays the loan, the company stock turns into cash or the entire effort fails. Once they are your financial partner, it is difficult to tell an Angel, for whatever reason, "please leave" or "we want our company back."

Angels have long memories. If you must cut off the business relationship with an Angel, "do not burn your bridges behind you." Here are some phrases for saying goodbye:

For Bankers and Commercial Loan Companies

Meet and talk with them so they understand why you wish to end the financial engagement.

> ➤ "I have come to pay off our loan earlier than we had agreed. I have also decided that some of your business practices and procedures do not fit mine. I trust we might do business under different circumstances in the future."

> ➤ "You have handled our account very well but now I would like to satisfy the loan note."

Deliver it in a business-like manner, maintaining civility and not finding fault.

With Private Angel Investors

It is difficult, if not impossible, to detach from this Angel. They have invested for the long term. If the company is moving forward, the private investor is very hesitant to sell their stock ownership position.

You could offer to buy their stock at its current value. However, a better use of that money is building the future of your enterprise. Here are useful phrases to disengage from these Angels:

"Our company has grown quite well since you first invested. Now the company wants to propose buying your stock position. There certainly has been an increase in value and we can negotiate a fair price for the stock."

OR, if the original investors are not capable of meeting your growth funding needs:

"Our growth level now demands an investor group whose resources can meet the funding challenges. Your early risk taking was and continues to be the best money to come into the enterprise. We have new interested investors who want our original investors bought out at a reasonable profit. I know this is an unusual situation. Would you entertain a sale of your stock proposal?"

OR, if an Angel is too demanding, say:

"Your attitudes about and impressions of your right to be involved in the day-to-day operations are unacceptable to me and the team. Your interference in our business is affecting company progress. We must find a way to purchase your stock. Here is what we propose ...."

Private investors like selling their investments at a profit so these approaches may work for detaching from this PathMaster

Family and Friends

Detaching from these Angels is the most manageable and easiest. Try this phrase:

"You were a great help when we first started. Now the company is entering an even more risky growth period and I want to be sure you get back what you put into the enterprise. So here is your original loan amount plus interest. The company has grown in value and you will receive what you invested for each stock share plus the amount of increased share value. I will make sure you get informal progress reports about how we doing. Thank you again."

Severing these relationships can be emotional so be careful of feelings.

To close other Angel relationships, such as suppliers, customers, governments, and commercial loan companies, use comments suggested for private investors and bankers. In all cases, be very sure you want to end the money connection. Then do it with tact and care.

CHAPTER FOURTEEN

O.k., Pathmasters - It's Your Turn

W E HAVE LEARNED HOW micropreneurs, founders, owners and company managers can work with a PathMaster to add value. At times, I suggested they be demanding and maybe confrontational. At other times, I recommended they be cooperative and open. Most importantly, I asked micropreneurs to look beyond their own capabilities by inviting you, the PathMaster, to support the business-building effort.

PathMasters, let me describe your working styles, skills, likes and dislikes. You each deal with issues differently, but I am confident my general views speak to all of you. Let us get started.

PROFILING THE MICROENTREPRENEUR

First, what are the common characteristics of a microenterprise founder and solo leader?

Well, literature describes them as lonely, under stress, perhaps too dedicated to their work, often at the expense of family. They relentlessly work towards potential financial gain or just personal survival, suspicious of outsiders, more autocratic than democratic, impatient, urgent, want to do it themselves, somewhat risk averse, and carry immense responsibility for their family, team of employees, community and country. This is all true. Most importantly, they are human engines creating an economically competitive and strong nation by bringing enterprises into existence and making them flourish. The future depends on their persistence, tenacity and courage.

U.S. President Calvin Coolidge's words surely apply to micropreneurs:

PRESS ON

"Nothing in this world can take the place of persistence. Talent will not; nothing is more common than unsuccessful people with talent. Genius will not; unrewarded genius is almost a proverb. Education will not; the world is full of educated derelicts. Persistence and determination alone are omnipotent. The slogan "press on" has solved and always will solve the problems of the human race."

Now to views about a micropreneur's personal and operating characteristics:

> They have distinctive mannerisms and styles, yet they are all the same

> They build up protective layers against criticism, doubt, disappointment, frustration, and inadequacy

> They differ in personality from outgoing and assertive, to withdrawn and passive

> They welcome alternatives and suggestions but do not immediately acknowledge them as useful

> They absorb the ideas of others, change them to become their ideas, and then act on them

SUGGESTING CONSTRUCTIVE IDEAS FOR THEM TO CONSIDER IS THE VITAL ROLE OF A PATHMASTER. ONLY WHEN THEY TAKE OWNERSHIP OF YOUR HELPFUL IDEA, WILL IT BE USEFUL FOR THE COMPANY.

> They rarely credit others for such contributions

> They are usually very frugal and spend money as if it were their own

- They oppose any ownership of their enterprise by others

- They prefer to manage alone

The Micropreneur's Vital Statistics:

- Starts a business, on average, between the ages of 25 to middle 60's

- Most are working at a business similar to the kind they want to start or grow

- Engineers and scientists start technology and complex product enterprises

- Sales people start simple product, service or retail enterprises

- Most are educated enough to reach the enterprise stage of customer sales

- Most are willing to delegate managing tasks when cash is flowing

- Some strive for wealth, others to reach their own capability, still others to build a comfortable and financially supportive enterprise

➤ Many typically avoid risk rather than chance failure, while many reach and risk just for the challenge

PathMasters, your client is quite a character. Take a minute to think about how you feel about working with these kinds of people. As you meet enough micropreneurs, you will see how similar they are to one another. Your goal is to understand their particular needs and to help move them through barriers so they may realize even more of their inborn talent, energy, and passion to succeed.

A CLOSER LOOK AT THE PATHMASTERS

The Mentor – Who Are You?

You are the force at the younger person's side. You have the wisdom, experience, tact and sensitivity to say just the right words at just the right time, energizing their confidence to act. You are there, but not interfering or doing. You are reliving your own career experiences through the micropreneur's passion and ego to succeed. When I say, "What is a mentor?" most people respond with "You know, a teacher, an elder, or coach, maybe a guide or friend." Well, I believe these descriptions are close but do not fit the profile of a mentor for a small enterprise founder.

For instance, a <u>teacher</u> is someone in a schoolroom where we, the learner, often just listen and take notes.

We respond to questions and dutifully turn in home-work. Seldom do we question a teacher's professorial perspectives or conclusions. The micropreneur will not react to instruction like a student. We must create the right rapport, tone, relevant business examples and allow them to react to any "lessons."

If not a teacher, maybe an elder like a father, mother, uncle or aunt, grandparent, or close relative. We go to elders for wise advice, inspiration and direction. Most times, we are shy and reluctant to describe our shortcomings or pro-fess our talents. Sometimes we fear a scolding or punish-ment should we challenge an elder's views. More often, we accept their instructions without question, and just do what an elder says. Micropreneurs will respectfully listen but seldom follow such elder advice because they respect-fully feel the elder is not relevant to today's times.

A counselor sits behind a large desk and gives advice, like an attorney or solicitor, tax accountant, insurance agent, or doctor. When asked a question they quickly respond with an answer. We follow their advice because we learned early that they are usually right. The micro-preneur dislikes just hearing what to do. They want to know why the advice applies and then to consider the alternatives. Then, they decide to act.

A coach is like someone on an athletic field repeat-edly showing and drilling us in order to master new skills. When we accomplish basic performance, they instruct us on how to improve. Mentors do not correct our methods in order to master skills. Micropreneurs do not want to learn by repetitive drill.

A guide is someone leading a tour or identifying nature signs along a country trail. We follow as a guide raises an umbrella leading the way. The micropreneur wants to know the dangers ahead and not be just a follower.

A friend is a peer. They listen but we do not tell them all that is on our mind. While we trust them, we are concerned they will not keep all we say just between us. We respect their opinions. We are about the same age and experience level. But does our friend sometimes tell us what they think we want to hear? Can we confidently rely on their advice? At some time, a mentor may become a friend but a friend usually cannot be a mentor. A mentor will tell us the truth about reality.

Yes, a Mentor has some characteristics of a teacher, elder, counselor, coach, guide and friend but a PathMaster Mentor brings the micropreneur more. No single description fits what you really do. Let us take a closer look.

A micropreneur needs a Mentor who is:

➤ older but not too old

➤ a patient listener and sensitive to all hopes and fears

➤ impartial and realistic, insightful and experienced in growing a business

➤ illuminating and reflecting back, suggesting, not showing or telling

> yielding not commanding, speaks directly, determined the micropreneur understands

> available to confer, trusted, transitional not permanent

> non-judgmental and prefers common sense to the theoretical

These styles make a good PathMaster Mentor. But "how can I act that way?" you say? Well, it takes work, concentration, commitment and patience.

A Mentor's natural instinct is demanding, persuasive and quick to respond. You like to take control and be decisive when leading others. You are convincing enough to get others to do what you want, when you want it done. A MENTOR DOES NOT AND MUST NOT ACT THIS WAY. Try to remember how you felt and reacted when you had to manage through challenges your younger venturer is now facing. Your helping behavior style must change. In doing so you will find this role exciting and very satisfying.

The Coach - Who Are You?

"We have a job to do, so let's get about doing it now." A coach's role is vital to improve enterprise functions during each forward stage of enterprise growth. You want action, and approach the microenterprise wearing a variety of hats: as trainer, consultant, instructor, teacher and facilitator. No matter what hat you wear, underneath you are a coach.

A Coach is engaging, asking, open, professional, and urgent. You are eager for everyone to learn skills. After following your guidance, you encourage your trainees. You are careful your coaching time be used efficiently. After conferring with the micropreneur, you are open to their suggested changes. You go to work and finish coaching on time, on budget, with the company's request to return for future work. <u>Micropreneurs really like a coach!</u>

The Expert - Who Are You?

Your special knowledge brings the micropreneur the real facts. Your manner is confident as you persuade all to hear the truth. You are not a coach nor are you a mentor. You probe, listen to questions, and define the unknown for others to seek.

An Expert is confident, superior, deliberate, challenging, sometimes cynical, and very businesslike. Driven to get good information, to execute fact finding and present task-specific search results. Insistent everyone hears and understands the reported observations, conclusions and recommendations.

Of all PathMasters, the Expert is the most insistent that the micropreneur face and understand outside reality. Their information forces and helps find creative solutions to build team confidence to reach beyond the present. Experts make fine contributions and take deep satisfaction in their work. Micropreneurs like how experts find and convey the right information.

The Angel - Who Are You?

Your cash is the lifeblood of the enterprise. All microventurers compete for your attention, enthusiasm and funding commitment. You take this vital business-building role and responsibility very seriously. You are tough-minded and relentless to gain the fairest and highest return.

As an Angel, you like:

> finding ways to be better involved with the micro-preneur and team

> having complete business plans before and after providing money

> truthful and timely sales reports and cost discussions

> knowledge of all problems causing missed plan targets and any warnings of potential negative competitive activity

As an Angel, you dislike:

> ➤ last minute changes or hesitancy after a financing agreement is reached

> ➤ financial needs offered to other Angels for better terms

> ➤ failing to meet agreed upon financial milestones

> ➤ finding out business forecasts contained weak facts and assumptions

> ➤ being unaware of team management changes

> ➤ being last to know about bad news and any negative business activity surprises

The Angel and micropreneur relationship is more productive when you listen closely and understand the barriers and opportunities as the micropreneur sees them, before you become convinced of their need for capital. You work hard to "stand in their shoes." Then, you build empathy, rapport and mutual trust, and praise the micropreneur for meeting the investment bargain.

How to know the relationship has matured:

➤ when you have mentally moved to the micro-preneur's side of the desk and become a true partner

➤ when words change from "I" or "my" to "we" and "our"

➤ when you get excited for their victories and offer comfort in defeats

➤ when you talk about increasing enterprise value rather than investor capital loss

➤ when your direct, open, tough-minded critique of enterprise issues changes their behavior and action

➤ when your continuous encouragement, sup-port, push, and urging cause the micropreneur and team to reach beyond their current capabilities

Angels are the success fulcrum for the enterprise, the community, and the nation. You are the lubricant for the engine of change and progress. <u>Micropreneurs need Angels as contributing and supporting financial partners.</u>

WORKING WITH THE MICROPRENEUR

Their Unique Enterprise

The words "but my business is different" will ring in your ears as you come to know a micropreneur. Remember, they are convinced their enterprise is unique. It is one of kind. Now, you and I know that is not true because we walked these same paths before with other micropreneurs. This "unique" attitude protects them from saying: (1) I do not have all the answers, (2) I do not want anyone telling me how to manage, or (3) what you suggest may require change, and change is risk. Their concerns are neither wrong nor invalid. They are what they are.

Here are some ways to break down defensive barriers:

> Tell short anonymous stories about companies that experienced similar "unique" problems or challenges.

> Ask "What do you consider is really different about your enterprise?" Then, "Why is it different than, well, the company in the next building?" and "What special challenges are you facing that others have not had to meet?"

> Step up to a black or white board. List the operational challenges micropreneurs feel are the most important to manage. Now ask, "I am going to put

a check beside those items you feel are unique to your business. Tell me which ones to check."

This questioning approach usually works, but not always. Try another way:

"Look, I know your company is absolutely no different than all the other firms I have worked with. And you are no different from the man or woman who run those other enterprises down the street. Your company is facing the very same problems as all the others have faced as they grew. Now let's start talking about your real issues."

Or, "Yes, the products are different, but every growing enterprise makes and sells products or services they think are different. Yes, customers are slightly different. Where they want to buy is different too. Every growing company has to find, persuade, sell and service customers. Yes, cash is tight. However, every growing company gets financing from somewhere. Yes, your employees are disappointing at times. But every company has to find the right people to grow. Yes, you and your team members are different, but believe me, you are really all more or less the same. Look, all of you either speak faster or slower, and wear different clothes. But all of you have a common goal to grow this microbusiness. You will or have already stumbled over, as others have, the same barriers along the start-up or growth path. So let us put aside difference as an excuse that cannot be helped. Let us go to work."

Use any words, gestures, or actions to cause realistic thinking. Move them towards accepting the experiences of others as useful to their venture. Consider this mind-changing work as your most crucial mission and challenge.

The Enterprise Life Cycle

Remember, your special competence is your experience walking the well-worn path to enterprise growth, maturity, or untimely sudden death. Being a prepared PathMaster is critical. Here are ideas to gauge where the enterprise is in its life cycle.

First, determine how far the enterprise has traveled along its path by using these general signposts:

> Ask them to describe, in general terms, the company status.

> Evaluate financial information, looking for sources of revenue and cost reductions.

> Discuss and compare market competitors.

> Gauge their outlook, objectives and attitudes compared to your experience with other micropreneurs at a similar business life stage.

> Determine whether the working environment is chaotic, urgent, organized, reactive, or busy and

focused. Look for clues such as how often the phones ring, interruptions for "urgent" decisions, work areas tidy or cluttered and if reception area magazines are current. These subtle signs tell a great deal about how the micropreneur manages the enterprise.

> Reach some early observations about the way the micropreneur is reacting to and answering your questions, and whether they are actively engaged in the discussion.

Your potential help must match the business life cycle that appeals to you and best uses your experience, style, and disposition. Carefully decide whether you fit. If yes, proceed. If no, withdraw. A poor fit will surely end badly.

Company Politics

No matter how large or small the enterprise, there exists a political dynamic. At every level, employees compete for their supervisor's favor. Likewise, team members seek special recognition and promotion from their family, the team, investors and shareholders. PathMasters must avoid becoming involved in enterprise politics.

Small enterprise management will always say there is no political or bureaucratic activity in their company. You will hear statements such as:

> "We are too small, have too much to do, and no time for those kinds of games."

> "I am not political and will not tolerate those attitudes."

> "Everyone knows I reward hard work and team play, I just don't see any activity suggesting politics."

They can say it, but there surely are politics in their hallways.

Let us see what is going on in small and larger enterprises.

Most always, a strong owner or CEO has less strong subordinates. Machiavelli, in the 16th century, taught us "a strong King has weak Barons." Because they are weaker than the King, Barons can only use political tactics to progress themselves. Machiavelli also says "a weak King has strong Barons," allowing plotting to either overthrow the weak king or cripple his authority and power. It is hard to imagine 16th century dynamics playing out in a 21st century small enterprise. Well, it does happen.

Often the founder or senior operating manager does not see, feel, comprehend, hear or can even imagine a political environment in their enterprise. This is because their ego clouds what is really going on between the "Barons" and themselves.

From the Barons, the PathMaster may hear these classic clues that politics are at play:

> "we are disorganized"

> "not enough resources"

> "not enough people to really do the job"

> "we are weak in certain areas ... such as...."

> "my opinion is, and the top person knows how I feel"

> "there seems to be friction among the team that is undermining our ...."

From the King, the PathMaster may hear:

> "There are times when some team members come to me and ...."

> "I have to watch them all the time or else they are at each other's throat."

> "Someone take my place? Not a chance."

> "Sure, I set up competition within my team, it makes them work harder."

They probably do see how destructive politics can be. Think about what the micropreneurs do. They create competition between Barons, allow private audiences, encourage gossip, and rule with an iron hand. Why do they do it? Mostly, so the Barons cannot "overthrow the King." It is quite normal and healthy to lead with a "strong hand" when an enterprise is very young. Managing the political activity level is not a PathMaster's work. Do not get involved.

PathMasters and Risk

Risk is reaching beyond the certain to connect with the uncertain. We all suffer anxiety when asked to move or act with certainty towards invisible or unclear futures. As a PathMaster, you have limited risk assisting an enterprise. Your reputation probably will not suffer by a failed outcome. On the other hand, your reward for a successful initiative will be a stronger reputation. There is just not much for you to lose or gain from the support asked of you.

Your task is to encourage a venturer to take reasonable and prudent risks. If they risk, enterprise growth accelerates. The micropreneur finds and hires new team members. The team matures to meet new challenges. Profitable sales occur. Creativity is unleashed to convert ideas into new products and services. In addition, the community and nation become more competitive. Supporting the microventurer to reach beyond their fears causes them to win, so then everyone wins. If they fail, at least everyone tried. Trying and failing is the nature of business.

A micropreneur builds the enterprise builds itself brick-by-brick, working long hours, with much stress, and mostly through trial and error. Micropreneurs are wary that outsiders will not keep their enterprise information confidential. Respect these real concerns and artfully relieve and remove their fear. They purposely hang double thick front doors so intruders do not disrupt what they are building.

Be a Believer

A micropreneur's uniqueness stems from extreme audacious persistence coupled with commitment, enthusiasm, and urgency. Without these personal traits, solid success will not occur. So, with their success-bound forecast numbers, their excited talk about how great it will be, their "arm waving" of product and service elegance, it is only believable when goals are met. PathMasters cannot mandate these micropreneur characteristics or passions. However, if you sense their lack of self-confidence is holding back their energy, then you must arouse and release their zeal to succeed. When you become a believer, you too will echo their vision and goals.

Do Not Feel Rejected

PathMasters usually bring realities that distort and disturb the microventurer's picture of the future. If your description of a new vision is too different from what they believe, then their perceived daily struggle may seem less possible or worthwhile. They guard against facing a premature reality by initially rejecting outsider opinions. Micropreneur phrases that signal their caution are:

> ➤ "I have thought it over. We have so many projects going on, now is just not the right time for us to embark on any new initiatives."

> ➤ "Cash flow is really tight. I think we should wait awhile before we begin."

> ➤ "I really want to see if our sales plans work and new supplier arrangements yield more profit. Then we will have a better idea of our future direction."

A PathMaster must accommodate these excuses. Your skills can only be effective when the time is right for the micropreneur. Keep suggesting they move forward, but wait for the micropreneur to decide the right time for themselves.

Getting Paid for Your Experience

There are no set fee schedules for PathMasters. Micropreneurs must agree to a fair and reasonable price or value for your performance. Just be open, practical, and fair.

Saying Goodbye

Whatever the reason, a PathMaster says goodbye with tact, understanding, and swiftness. Always leave all the doors open for a return to help the micropreneur.

CHAPTER FIFTEEN

THAT WRAPS IT UP!

S UMMARIES ARE TEDIOUS. Here are some final vital thoughts.

For you, the Micropreneur:

➤ Your enterprise will evolve through life cycles. Now recognize that personally you will too.

➤ You thought you could do all the work. Now use all the outside help you can get.

➤ You thought your business situation unique and different from all others. Now believe it is not.

➤ Your concerns about losing control, abilities to make it happen, keeping your business information secret, and risk and reward assumptions were valid. Now consider them less important than you imagined.

> You had doubt about outsiders. Now go find, hire, work with, reward and discharge PathMasters.

> You felt overwhelmed to compete in an ever-changing marketplace. Now go meet the challenges and exploit the opportunities.

For You, the PathMaster

> You have the skills and wisdom produced by trial and error. Now give them to younger business builders.

> You have met, yet again, the typical microventurers who differ only in how they say things, dress, and react. Now make them feel at ease that you too have been where they are.

> You understand their personal concerns about inside information, remaining in full control and being self-confident. Now work with them using empathy, wisdom, experience, practicality, and prudence.

> You are sensitive to their managing style. Now adjust your style and behavior to fit theirs.

For Micropreneurs and PathMasters

You learned how to talk to each other about many subjects, now say:

> You know value received requires value returned. Now find a fair working arrangement.

> <u>You see the advantages of working together. Now go to work!</u>

Appendix One

** QUESTIONS PATHMASTERS ASK AND MICROVENTURERS MUST ANSWER

Who, what, where, which, when, how much and how many frame the questions most asked by PathMasters. Micropreneurs, your answers tell others what and how much you know. Get prepared for questions from the Coach, Expert, and Angel. Study the following mostly marketing oriented questions you may be asked by a PathMaster. Make notes of your answers.

PRODUCT OR SERVICE PERFORMANCE:

> how do you define products and services your customers will buy?

> how do you identify new product features?

> how do you secure new products, set sales forecasts?

- how many sizes, shapes, colors do customers want to buy?

- how much change has the customer demanded in quality?

- how much time does it take customers to assemble your product?

- how do you define new products?

- how do you get information to define a new product or service?

- what changes in product reliability are customers expecting?

- what is the customer using now for their needs?

- what products/services give the enterprise the most revenue and profit?

- what new product, benefit or service would the customer prefer?

- what performance is added or changed?

- when is product/service training and maintenance expected by the customer?

> where is or how does the customer gain value from your services?

PRICE:

> how do you set prices according to what customers will pay?

> how do you find the right price to charge?

> how much will customers pay?

> how much money is spent to buy all similar goods and services?

> how much detail is needed in customer price or work proposals?

> how much will a customer willingly pay for change?

> how do you find the highest price that customers will pay?

> how do you determine product bestseller inventory levels?

> how do you determine the current total market available to you?

- what is the typical warranty for products/services like yours?

- what competitive price and performance approach is best for your business?

- when does product/service performance have to pay back the price paid?

- what is the break-even price to remain profitable?

- what is the lowest price needed to meet competitors' prices?

DISTRIBUTION:

- how do you change the business offerings to get more traffic?

- how do you expand your business and locate new customers?

- how do you find new distribution channels?

- how do you select the best distribution to reach customers?

- how do they want after-sale service changed?

> how do you know where people want to buy new products?

> how many units do customers usually buy at one time?

> how many units does the total market buy?

> how much does each distribution channel cost to reach customers?

> how much margin does the distribution channel expect?

> how does finding new resellers for your products expand business revenue?

> how do you identify new distribution channels?

> what after-sale service and training does the customer expect?

> what do customers like or dislike about your service?

> what is the current distribution channel for products/services?

> what other distribution method would they prefer, for example an online catalog?

- what distribution changes will be required to meet your profit goal?

- when is the peak buying time of day?

- where are the large and smaller customers located?

- where do customers usually visit to buy products/ services like yours?

- where do customers learn how to use or fix your product?

- who, in the distribution chain, does the customer prefer?

- why should resellers buy, stock, demonstrate and sell our goods and services?

CUSTOMERS:

- how do you define after-sale service needs?

- how do you determine available market potential?

- how do you find and attract new customers?

- how do customers decide about shopping in a certain store?

- how much does a bank usually allow the business to borrow?

- how much cash is needed for near term operation, inventory, advertising, etc.?

- how quickly do customers want product or service delivery?

- what are the major trade or consumer venues to shop?

- what media do potential customers use - internet, newspaper, radio, T.V.?

- what does the customer expect in after-sale support?

- what does the customer really think about your products/service?

- what information do you have to fix a problem?

- what are the customer's criteria for making a buying decision?

- what is the perceived difficulty people have using the product instructions?

- what do customers think about the value of your products or services?

- when must a product or service innovation be available for the market?

- when does the customer usually buy products/services like yours?

- when is the typical delivery of product/service expected?

- where is the customer using your product or the competitors?

- which advertising medium or shop merchandising attracts customers?

- who, at the customer's business, is the end user?

- who, at the customer's business, specifies product/service performance?

- who, at the customer's business, makes the buying decision?

- who, at the customer's business, wants a supplier change?

- why do customers just look around the shop and do not buy?

COMPETITION:

> how do you identify competitive technologies or services that may replace yours?

> how do you learn about and track competition?

> how do the new competitors know what the customer really wants?

> how many employees are moving to your competitor's place of business?

> how many people enter a competitor's shop per hour or per day?

> how much revenue and profit are your competitors getting?

> how many units is each of your major competitors selling?

> how much will these low-cost suppliers drive prices down?

> how can you cause the customer to think of you as better than the competition?

> how do you track competition?

- what is the competition doing?

- what are the barriers to entry for a new supplier?

- what are the perceived good and bad points of competition?

- what distribution methods will competition use?

- what does the customer really think about your competitors?

- what purchasing policies do you have for buying from only one supplier?

- what is the competitive technology or service to replace you?

- what is the current level of competition?

- what product/service is needed to replace what the customer uses?

- what share of all shoppers prefers your store to local competition?

- what do customers like or dislike about your shop compared to a competitor?

- what is needed to change your product or service performance?

- when will a replacement technology or service be available?

- when will you have to do business differently because of new technology?

- when will your customers buy similar, lower priced products somewhere else?

- where do customers buy product/services similar to yours?

- which vendors are delivering goods to competition?

- who is the current competition?

- who is the potential competition?

- who are the competitor's major customers?

- who are the competitor's salespersons who call on your customers?

- why do customers buy from your competitors?

- why does competition use the distribution channels they do?

- why does the customer need more than one supplier?

- why do customers buy from competition?

OTHER MARKETING ACTIVITIES:

- what business are you really in?

- how do you communicate your business story?

- how do you locate import or export opportunities?

- how long do you engage a consultant to work on problems?

- how do you create potential customer traffic and sales leads?

- how do you differentiate your business?

- how long does it take to collect your receivables?

- how many sales calls does it take to get an order?

- how many times do customers expect you to visit them in a month?

- how much do you typically pay a marketing consultant, per hour or per day?

- ➤ how do you plan to change the business?

- ➤ how do you close more sales?

- ➤ how do you determine the total market potential?

- ➤ what advertising is most effective to pull customers into your business?

- ➤ what is the market intelligence plan to get this information?

- ➤ when is the normal payment period for supplier and customer invoices?

- ➤ where and from whom do customers want to hear your selling proposition?

- ➤ who are the industry opinion leaders and experts?

- ➤ why are sales leads from your promotions so few, many or worthless?

** Questions are from *"Marketing Intelligence, Discover What Your Customers Really Want and What Your Competitors Are Up To,"* Author: *Jack Savidge, Published by Business One Irwin, 1992; Jack Savidge & Company 2001.*

Appendix Two

ALL ABOUT VENTURE CAPITALISTS

Professional Venture Capitalists (VC's)

Venture Capitalists (VC's) manage capital from large pension funds and wealth sources for investment in small enterprises. Historically, venture capital investing rewards are greater than traditional stocks or bonds.

The VC invests to obtain ownership in a firm that over time will significantly increase in value. Each capitalist invests in different stages of enterprise growth. Some prefer (Stage 1) idea to proof of concept, (2) start up or commercial launch, (3) growth and first profit, and (4) later stage, before sale or public offering of the enterprise. Stage 1 investments are the highest risk but the highest returns. Each following stage offers lower risk and reduced rewards. You can find interested VC's during any of your company's life stages.

VC Investment Reality

Long established VC industry facts (found on the internet) will prepare you to meet a VC Angel. All venture capitalists say they only invest in potential "winners." What else would a professional investor select? However, when evaluating their investment portfolio five to seven years later, not all companies are winners. The investment portfolio results change over time, moving from all winners into three categories: winners, the living dead, and losers.

A winner has returned more than 10 times (10X) the original investment. That is, for every unit of money put in the VC collected 10 units. A living dead company is still operating but at the most may return 2 times (2X) the investment, someday. A loser has returned zero capital and has closed its doors.

The VC Investing Process

Assume that a VC originally reviews 500 investment opportunities. Just 10% or 50 ventures are seriously considered. They invest in only 2% or 10 of those originally reviewed. The future rewards from the 10 investments were far more than the risks taken. Remember, when a VC invested their money they were only investing in a "winner." Here is what really happened.

> These 10 firms received an investment in year 1. It is now 5 years later. By now, the portfolio has suffered 5 loser ventures for a zero return. There are now 5 left. Of these, 3 living dead show no signs for potential growth but have a cash flow allowing marginal survival. So, should the 2 remaining be winners?

➤ Now it is the 7th year. The 3 living dead remain alive but growth prospects are still dim. Between the 2 potential winners, 1 was purchased by a larger firm returning the VC 10 times their original investment. The other winner company went on the public stock market, returning 20 times their investment.

The final return arithmetic may be helpful. Let us assume money equal to 1,000 invested in each of 10 ventures.

➤ Investment in the 10 = 10,000
  (1,000 x 10)
                           Return
➤ 5 losers at 0 X return =   0

➤ 3 living dead at 2X =   6,000
  (3 at 1,500)

➤ 1 winner at 10X =   10,000

➤ 1 winner at 20X =   20,000

Total Return 10 = <u>36,000 or 3.6X</u>

This VC portfolio investment return example reflects decades of industry statistics. This Angel cannot loosen their risk investment selection rules or minimum reward goals. Why? Because the future portfolio return rate would surely be lower if they are less prudent in their selections. They must only invest in a winner they perceive will return 20X or more. The burden is on you to convince them your company is a winner.

Now you understand why VC's ask for or demand a high percentage of company ownership for their investment money. They want more of tomorrow's reward to offset today's risk. They know they will have living dead and loser investments. Those losses must be offset with high winner rewards. You may get angry when the VC wants so much ownership. But move forward, you and the VC are working toward the same success goals. There is an old saying, "**take the money.**"

Here is what you can expect when financially partnering with professional venture capitalists:

Your Advantages:

> capital you do not have to pay back

> experienced advice to solve problems

> meeting other micropreneurs the VC has funded

> an experienced member for your Board of Directors

Your Disadvantages:

> ➤ VC's own a large part of your company, you own less

> ➤ VC's ownership power interferes with your decisions

> ➤ VC's right to take control if you can no longer manage

It is a difficult decision to accept VC money. However, for the long-term probability of success, consider the VC investment to help you reach your vision. This statement applies to having a VC partner – "It is far better to own a smaller share of bigger enterprise than 100% of nothing." This Angel PathMaster is an experienced financial and business manager who always adds more value than just their money.

Appendix Three

STRATEGIC IMPERATIVES AS THE ENTERPRISE GROWS

Unless a microventure owner or manager truly believes the enterprise must change to grow, change will not happen. So, the PathMaster's mission is to encourage, not insist, think strategically, create new goals and identify what is best and how to change.

As a PathMaster, a first step is to ask micropreneurs, "What business are you really in?" This simple but penetrating question forces a more realistic and precise company description. Probe the answer for the real issues to stimulate ideas about how to meet an uncertain future. Uncertainty focuses attention on business survival and profit alternatives. Together the search for doable solutions begins.

Engage the microventurer and team and ask them to answer these questions for each strategic imperative:

IMPERATIVE 1 - <u>WORSHIPPING YOUR CUSTOMERS</u>

> ➤ "When was the last time you personally visited your key customers?"

> ➤ "Did you thank them for their business?"

> ➤ "What did they say after you asked how you could better serve them?"

IMPERATIVE 2 - <u>SEIZING MONEY, IDEAS & PEOPLE NOW - NOT LATER</u>

> ➤ "Do you really have enough money to reach your next milestone?"

> ➤ "What new business ideas did you consider or pursue this past year?"

> ➤ "People make things happen. What are you doing to find and hire new talent?"

IMPERATIVE 3 - <u>REPLACE YOURSELF BEFORE COMPETITORS DO</u>

> ➤ "Assume competition has the money to develop a similar product or service."

> "Could they add better product or service features than yours?"

> "How much time would it take for competition to offer what and how you sell?"

> "What could you do to delay them from doing it?"

IMPERATIVE 4 - <u>SELL REGIONALLY, NATIONALLY</u> and <u>GLOBALLY</u>

> "Local customers are good but where else is revenue growth available?"

> "Why are you not set up to sell in these larger revenue potential markets?"

IMPERATIVE 5 - <u>BECOME THE LOW COST PRODUCER</u>

> "When and why will the prices go down on products or services like yours?"

> "When they do fall, will your cost to produce be low enough to compete?"

> "What do you see as major cost reduction opportunities?

IMPERATIVE 6 - FIND A MARKET GIANT THEN MAKE A FRIEND

> ‣ "It seems your new product or service can satisfy larger markets. However, your company is so small. What ideas do you have to enter these markets?"

> ‣ "If you do not meet customer needs, someone else will. Are there potential selling or manufacturing business partners in these new market areas?"

IMPERATIVE 7- BUILD A TEAM NOT AN ORGANIZATION CHART

> ‣ "The way you and your people manage change will improve employee efficiency and morale, and the delivery of quality products or services. Your company is a bit small to consider big operational changes. Yet, I do notice the decision making structure could be more efficient. How comfortable would you be to have others responsible for certain business functions like finance, marketing and customer service?"

IMPERATIVE 8 - KILL THE LOSERS AND FUEL THE WINNERS

> ‣ "You told me that a product/service idea you personally created is still being developed. When

will you start selling it? Will it be too late for the market?"

> "I have another question. The sales records show some items are not selling well. Why do you continue to spend money improving or stocking them? What is your reason for keeping items that are not growing? Why not take that money to support items that really show marketplace promise?"

IMPERATIVE 9 – EVANGELIZE THE VISION AND CULTURE

> "While meeting with your people, I randomly asked, 'tell me where you think the business is going?' Their replies were interesting. Some mentioned how they enjoyed the sense of fairness, of having a real team or family spirit, and echoed your shared future purpose and goals. You have created a team who enjoys their work and each other." Then ask the micropreneur, "Tell me, how did you get everyone to see and share your vision of the future?"

IMPERATIVE 10 - THINK STRATEGIC, ACT ENTREPRENEURIAL

> "I have been listening to what you think are the enterprise's crucial challenges. I hear you define the 'future' as two months from now. Sure, you

have daily fires to put out. But when do you take proper time to consider the company's future opportunities, the direction it must take and new goal setting?"

> "We talked about licensing a product patent or copyright from others. You said, 'I cannot think about that now, maybe later.' Suppose by not acting now you lose that product and market opportunity. I'd like your views."

While listening to their answers, consider asking two penetrating questions.

First, **"How do you know that?"** Do not ask "Why do you say that?" or "What makes you think that?" but "How do you know that?" These five simple words pierce the strongest armor.

Second, **"If money was no object, what ONE problem or challenge would you want solved?"** Lack of money prevents the microventurer from exploring all alternatives. So this question removes money as a barrier to action and will open their thinking.

The imperatives are intense. Your questions are direct. But when asked in a non-judgmental way, discussions will surely uncover the micropreneur's core issues, fears, and determination to succeed.

Appendix Four

A MENTOR - NEW DEFINITIONS FROM MANY LANDS

Foreign language dictionaries have many definitions of a Mentor, ranging from the mentor described in Homer's *The Iliad* or to a counselor or advisor. I described my new definition of a Mentor, presented in this book, with articulate individuals who are native speakers of various countries. Here are translated definitions for "Mentor."

FRENCH

The French version of our new mentor is:

"Un mentor est une personnne: en qui on a confiance; un auditeur patient; qui ne juge pas; eclairant et reflechissant; ayant du bon sens, pas theorique; complaisant, ne commandant pas; perspicace; plus age mais pas trop age; transitionnel, pas permanent; impartial et realiste; sensible aux inquietudes et aux peurs; aynat de l'experience dans l'evolution des affaires; qui suggere mais ne montre pas et ne dit pas; direct dans le dialogue; qui persevere pour comprendre."

GERMAN

A German dictionary translates "mentor" as "treuer" Ratgerber or Berater, or Mentor. Again, with someone skilled in the German language, I described the mentor characteristics I believe most suited to work with managing directors. Here is the German composite provided:

"Ein Mentor is jemand der 10 bis 20 Jahre alter ist, einen gesunden Menschenverstand besitzt, frei von Vorurtellen ist, seinen Studenten wichtig nimmt und bedinnungslos aktzepiert; geduldig, aufklarend und feinfuhlih ist, aber auch kritisch, uberlegend, einsichtsvoll und direkt und vollig vertrauend seinem Studenten eine freie Hand fur entscheidungen gewahrt."

SPANISH

Here is the Spanish definition for mentor:

"Un mentor es alguien que: sea confiable; sepa escuchar; no prevusque; nos de una refleccion realista; tenga sentido comun no teorico; sea complaciente, no dominante; sea perspicaz; sea mayor, en anos, pero no demasidado; sea transitorio, no permanente; y sea imparcial y realista.

FINNISH

The Finnish language describes a mentor as being a teacher, counselor, and director of plays. I asked several learned Finns to find exactly the right word or words that capture the mentor role in small business. We tried elder, counselor, teacher, uncle, godfather and the Finnish

word "mentori." They all fell short. So the phrase most closely describing a person we are going learn about is:
"Kokenut, vanhempi, henkio, joka valottaa tilannetta puolueettomasti".

ITALIAN

"Mentori" again surfaces as the Italian word for mentor and carries a defintion for advisor or counselor. The tone of the meaning is "godfather," or uncle. Here is the Italian description:
"Una perosona inelligente, provvista di sensibilita ed esperienza che, attraverso una combinazione di ascolto paziente e saggio consiglio, confidenza completa e nessuna critica, dedica la sua ispirazione, incoraggiamento, consiglio e guida ad una perosna piu giovane allo scopo di dirigere il suo protetto alla realizzazione di mete positive e soddisfacenti."

THE END